DAM Survival Guide

Things to know (and avoid) when designing, promoting and maintaining the perfect digital asset management initiative.

By David Diamond

For Skamook

Contact the author:
Blog: DAMSurvivalGuide.com
Google+: +DAM Survival Guide
Twitter: @DAMSurvival
Email: david@DAMSurvivalGuide.com

CreateSpace Edition
November, 2012 (v1)

Table of Contents

How This Book Can Help You

The Digital Asset Management (DAM) industry includes millions of users, hundreds of software developers, countless blogs, scores of industry analysts, a handful of trade show promoters, a few dedicated foundations and, now, a book that aims to help you survive it all.

The fact is, when done right, DAM can help organizations save time and money, better leverage their investments in digital assets, and even avoid litigation. And when done wrong, DAM can cause production delays, destroy creative workflows, frustrate users, and ultimately cost millions.

DAM is so deeply integrated into core business processes today that most experts agree the best way to increase your chances of digital asset management success is to wrap DAM into a corporate initiative you design, manage, deploy and promote exactly as you would if you were a software developer releasing a new product.

And you know what? That's exactly what you'll become.

DAM Survival Guide takes you through the entire process. From knowing what you can be doing right now, early in your research, to knowing what you should be doing at every step of the way.

You'll learn the basics of DAM. You'll see examples of how DAM can be a benefit or a hindrance, and you'll even read an entire chapter that tries to talk you out of pursuing digital asset management.

If after that you're still convinced that DAM is for you, DAM Survival Guide will help you:

- Know how to best determine your organization's DAM needs.
- Understand what you can reasonably expect from a DAM.
- Cut through the marketing-speak you hear from DAM vendors.
- Be ready and able to plan a DAM initiative that can succeed.

If you think that digital asset management is primarily about DAM software, you're reading this book just in time.

My name is David Diamond. I first started working with digital asset management in 1998. In all the years since, I've seen DAM succeed and fail on hundreds of occasions. And while the reasons for success were varied, the reasons for failure were all too often similar.

I wrote DAM Survival Guide to help organizations avoid these common pitfalls. In particular, I speak to *you*, the person charged with making DAM work at your organization.

There's a lot for you to know, and you probably don't have a lot of time to learn it all. And if you feel like you have to approach this massive DAM topic without a lot of support, I'm hopeful you've just found the first friend you'll need.

Let's get started.

What's the DAM Fuss?

If managing digital assets is such a great idea, why would there be so much concern over doing it successfully? Wouldn't DAM be something all organizations and users would adopt with great enthusiasm?

In a word, no.

Digital asset management is like dental floss. With daily use, the long-term benefits are significant. DAM and flossing share another misfortune in that the full benefits they offer aren't realized immediately. In fact, going through the motions of managing digital assets (digital flossing) is often inconvenient and tedious, at best.

Users hate things that are inconvenient and tedious, just like kids do.

The employees of an organization can be compared to kids. No matter how many times mom tries to explain why flossing is important, Xbox is *always* more fun. Even if the world's coolest dentist was to explain how great the long-term benefits of flossing will be, Facebook offers benefits today.

People prefer instant gratification for their efforts.

I've even tried to explain to resistant users that DAM is a selfless act we do for the benefit of others. I explain that while we know where *our* files are, we need to organize and tag them so that *others* can find what they need.

But honestly, this Good Samaritan approach rarely works.

The best method I've seen for motivating naysayer (or lazy) DAM users is similar to the most effective parenting tactic I've ever seen: coercion and manipulation.

Enter the DAM initiative, and what you need to know about it.

Asking for More Help

If you ever get stuck and want the guidance of DAM professionals you can trust, I'll provide whatever referrals I can. I'm not available for hire, myself, but there are people in this industry whom I consider to be knowledgeable and honest. I'm sure they'll do right by you, so I'm happy to make any connections I can.

Contact me:

- LinkedIn: http://www.linkedin.com/in/airdiamond
- Email: david@DAMSurvivalGuide.com

Let's Talk Terminology

If DAM is new to you, there are a few key terms you'll need to know in order to follow this or any other discussion on the topic. The definitions I give below are not taken from any official source; they are the definitions I've come up with for myself during my 14+ years working in the field.

I could have provided some official definitions, but most of the definitions I've heard just confuse me, so I ignore them.

Digital Asset Management

Rephrasing what's explained in the previous section, digital asset management, or DAM, describes the policies, practices and software an organization uses to manage its digital assets.

If the concept of managing a digital asset is foreign to you, it's helpful to compare *digital* asset management to *physical* asset management.

My favorite example is delivery trucks. We see FedEx and other delivery trucks every day. And while we might be focused more on the goodies they contain than the trucks themselves, somewhere there are policies, practices and software in use to manage those trucks.

FedEx wants to know where each truck is at any moment. They also want to know what each truck contains, who's driving it, when it's due for maintenance and, of course, they need to make sure each truck is properly registered with local governments.

When you're talking about thousands of delivery vehicles worldwide, and then you throw aircraft into the mix, it's easy to see why the company would need policies, practices and software in place to manage it all.

Now let's get back to digital asset management. For many organizations, images, brochures, media releases, videos and presentations are just as valuable as those trucks and airplanes are to FedEx. Just as FedEx carefully monitors the history, current statuses and futures of its vehicles, organizations use DAM to enable them to do the same with their digital assets. (It's not surprising that FedEx also uses DAM to manage the many logos, brochures, signs and signage it produces.)

Consider the follow table, which draws some parallels.

Physical Asset Management	Digital Asset Management
Where is the truck now?	Where is the file now?
When was the truck last serviced, and who performed that service?	When was the file last edited, and who edited it?
When is the truck due for maintenance?	When will the file need to be updated?
Who is authorized to perform maintenance on the truck?	Who can edit the file?
Who must approve the maintenance before the truck is returned to service?	Who must approve the edits before the file can be released?
When is the truck due for registration?	When will file's license expire?
How does the truck contribute to the company's bottom line?	How does the file contribute to the company's bottom line?

While it's safe to assume FedEx uses software to help it manage its fleets, it's also safe to assume policies and practices are in place too. After all, we live in an analog world in which truck drivers aren't apps—they need to know how to drive the truck, and they need to know the company's rules.

Likewise, digital asset management *software* is only one component of a greater (and smarter) digital asset management *initiative*. This is why it's important to define and perfect your DAM initiative on paper before you choose software.

▶ *It took more than 10 years before I was willing to use the term "DAM" to mean digital asset management (the practice) and digital asset manager (the software), as in, "Does your organization use a DAM?" Forgive me the inaccuracy, but the industry has beaten better judgment out of me on this point.*

Content vs. Files

At the root of the entire DAM discussion is the concept of *content vs. files*. The distinction can be subtle, but it's important to understand the difference.

Consider a single computer file that contains the Apple logo. That file contains intellectual property—*the content*—that's worth billions. But how valuable is that particular *file*? In truth, it's worthless. If you deleted the file, several million copies of the same content would continue to exist.

If you held the very last copy of the Apple logo available anywhere in the world, that file would be valuable, but this, of course, isn't a realistic scenario. If you knew you held the last copy of the Apple logo, you'd duplicate it, killing your file's uniqueness and billion dollar value.

Also consider a PDF version of an InDesign document. The InDesign file remains useful while the content is being edited, but once that content is ready for distribution, the PDF becomes the more important file. (Assuming updates won't be required.)

What this example shows is that it's common for the *content lifecycle* to exceed any given asset's lifecycle. For this reason, DAM software and initiatives that are more content focused are usually more in line with what users want and expect. For example, some DAM systems would treat those InDesign and PDF files as completely separate objects, while smarter DAMs would offer you a way to manage them both as a single entity.

This in mind, it's reasonable to ask why DAM is *file*-centric instead of *content*-centric. Shouldn't it be digital content management instead of digital asset management?

There are two reasons we continue to focus on files over content:

• Access

- Control

Until a time when files are no longer our primary liaisons to content, we'll think in terms of files, even though we care most about content. DAM enables us to access the files we need that contain the content we want.

Think about what happens when you order something online: Your focus immediately becomes the box. Has the box shipped? When will the box arrive? Once the box does arrive, you tear into it and cast it aside, as you shift your focus to the gadget (content) inside.

Poor box.

When it comes to digital content, files are nothing more than the boxes in which content is stored and shipped.

But the day when we no longer need to ship content is near. Think about Google Docs. When you share a Google Doc, you don't make a copy of the file; instead, Google sends a link to those with whom you want the content shared.

Social media is similar. When we share tweets or posts with others, we don't download files and attach them to email; we send links to the content. A billion people can see the same content without the need to duplicate it even once.

Sure, that content is stored somewhere in something you could consider to be a file. But the distinction is that we never directly touch that file as we manipulate, distribute and share the content it contains.

Then there's the issue of control. Anything worth having is worth preventing others from getting—that's human nature.

When we place a completed media release under an embargo, our intention is to prevent the file's content from being distributed. Our DAM enables us to meet that end by placing a lock on files that contain the media release content until the embargo has expired.

As long as there are digital files in the world, we'll need software that can control those files. So, even as we move closer to a content-focused world, we won't see the last of DAM until computers no longer store files, or until there are no computers at all.

What's a Digital Asset?

I like to define what a digital asset is by describing what it isn't. I think this puts the topic in much better focus. For the sake of discussion, let's say that anything not worthy of being a *digital asset* is merely a *digital file.*

A digital file has no meaningful history or future, and it poses no benefit or threat to your organization. Say, you create an invitation for an office cupcake fest to celebrate an employee's anniversary. That invitation will be useful for only a brief period, and it poses no tangible benefit or threat to your organization. In other words, this isn't a digital asset. (Sorry to sound so harsh; I'm sure your invitations are wonderful.)

On the other hand, you might be working on an annual report packed with great news for investors. That report will not only provide value to your organization when it's released, it will provide value in the future. Further, if it leaks out ahead of the mandated release date, it could unfairly manipulate your stock price and land you in court. The content of that report must be managed throughout its lifetime. That means that every file that contains that content must also be managed, making those files worthy of the term digital asset.

Another way of looking at the difference is to consider replacement cost. If the only copy of your invitation was lost *after* cupcake day, you probably wouldn't bother recreating it. If the only copy of your annual report was lost, you'd be required to recreate it, regardless of the cost.

If you're unsure about whether certain content provides any value, consider the costs and requirements associated with replacing that content.

In addition, many organizations generate direct revenue from their digital assets. Stock photo and film houses come to mind, but many companies also sell books, movies and other types of digital content that's delivered to users via files.

As mentioned, don't lose site of the potential for liability assets can present. Any file that would compromise or embarrass your organization if released, or simply released at the wrong time, should also be considered a digital asset that must be controlled.

Metadata Explained

Metadata is information that relates in some way to a given digital asset. In a nutshell, think about your mother. If someone was to ask you to describe her, explain how she was doing and say where she lived, all the information you provided would be metadata about the human asset you call mom. That information would not *be* your mother; it would just describe her condition, her location, etc.

▶ *The singular form of metadata, metadatum, is rarely used. For this reason, I use "metadata" when referring to both forms throughout this book.*

The most common types of metadata are keywords that describe a file's content. For example, the file contains a *flower* that's *red* and of the family *Rosaceae*.

Metadata is also used to describe aspects of a file other than its content. Who created the file? Who needs to approve it? When should it be released? All information used to describe content's history and future would be metadata. In addition, all information that describes the file itself—it's size, format, location, etc.—is also metadata.

I like to think of metadata as content's life story—a timeline of sorts. On the left, you have historical information. On the right, is the information that describes (or controls) the content's future. Right in the middle of the timeline is the information that describes the current state of the content and the file it's stored within.

Take a look at this table of example metadata values.

Historical Metadata	Current Metadata	Future Metadata	File Metadata
Creator	Production status	Approved Editors	Name
Creation date	Location	Next update	Size
Cost of development	Current editor	Usage restrictions	Format
Directive	Keywords	License	Location

	expiration		
Licensees	Language	Target audience	Date Created

Historical metadata describes the origin of content, and all the things that have happened to that content since it was developed. This might include the creator, the original directive that described the work to be done, and even a list of customers to whom the content has been licensed. As a matter of practice, these metadata values should not be changed once they've been an official part of the content's history. This is a great example of how policy can help ensure the integrity of your metadata.

Current metadata describes the status of the content at the moment, including where it's stored, the keywords that describe it and its language. Take note that while some "current" metadata changes over the content lifecycle (status, editor), some values are unlikely to change. Language is an example, as are the keywords used to describe the content.

Future metadata describes plans, limitations or expectations in place for the content. These values are typically subject to change. Some "future" values, like next-update date, can be become historical data, if they're worth keeping at all. Or, you might simply find that you overwrite the values once they become obsolete, without keeping a historical record of previous values. This is another matter of policy.

File metadata values describe the file itself. They are usually provided by the applications and operating systems used to create the content. Users will definitely want to see and search on these values, but they won't be editing them directly very often. An exception to this is file name, which you might change from time to time via your DAM.

With the exception of file metadata, most of the metadata values you enter will apply equally to all files that contain the content. For example, if your DAM stores copies of a master file in different formats (derivatives), the copyright and usage restrictions assigned to that content are likely the same for all those derivatives. This is where a DAM that enables you to manage different versions and derivatives of a file in a single database record can really save you some time, and help ensure proper metadata values are associated with all containers of that content.

When designing your DAM initiative, keep these metadata distinctions in mind. They'll help you keep things organized, and they can also help you ensure you have all the metadata fields you'll need to adhere to the policies you define.

Even better, metadata classifications can help you manage some administrative aspects of your DAM. For example, permissions are easier to manage when it's easy to determine which metadata values should be editable or visible to each user.

For example, say your policy mandates that the only users who can edit historical metadata are trusted writers who can correct typos, while leaving the original meaning of the metadata intact. Policy might additionally require that all usage restrictions be controlled by Legal, or that all decisions with regard to audience suitability are made by Marketing.

When your metadata fields adhere to classifications you understand, it's easier to be able to adhere to policies like these. They also make the process of adding new metadata fields to your DAM easier (and safer) too. If all you need to determine for a new field is what class of metadata it will contain, you'll know exactly which users should have read and edit access to that field, because your policy will dictate it.

Taxonomies and Controlled Vocabularies

To help rein in the virtually infinite (and ambiguous) keyword possibilities that exist, organizations create or adopt taxonomies, controlled vocabularies, or both. These concepts put some structure and limits on the tags used, making assets easier to categorize and find.

A taxonomy is like a hierarchy of agreed upon, approved or otherwise standardized keywords. Consider the following example for the categorization of vehicles.

- Air > Airplane > Jet-powered > Cargo
- Air > Airplane > Jet-powered > Passenger
- Air > Airplane > Prop-powered > Cargo
- Air > Airplane > Prop-powered > Passenger
- Ground > Automobile > Luxury > Rolls Royce
- Ground > Automobile > Luxury > Jaguar
- Ground > Automobile > Sport > Jaguar
- Ground > Automobile > Sport > Ferrari

- Ground > Service > Construction > Tractor
- Ground > Service > Construction > Cement Mixer
- Ground > Service > Municipal > Fire Engine
- Ground > Service > Municipal > Police Car
- Sea > Powered > Purpose > Water Skiing
- Sea > Powered > Purpose > Personal Recreation
- Sea > Sail > Purpose > Personal Recreation

A hierarchically structure like this enables users to assign digital assets to the outermost topics, knowing an association with parent topics is implied.

For example, when an asset is assigned to the *Rolls Royce* topic, it can also be found by those searching for all *Ground* vehicles, all *Ground > Automobile* vehicles, and all *Ground > Automobile > Luxury* vehicles.

This hierarchical structure alleviates users from having to make each of those sub-topic assignments manually. Plus, the standardized structure gives metadata editors and users, alike, something consistent with which they can become familiar over time. This, of course, improves workflow efficiency.

Some organizations create their own taxonomies, while others adopt taxonomies created by others. The US Library of Congress publishes a massive taxonomy that many organizations use. (They use the term "Subject Headings" to describe this service.)

US Library of Congress taxonomy products contain thousands of topics, which can be overwhelming, but it enables organizations like libraries and other institutions that work with public assets to offer some cross-organizational standard. In other words, by using the same taxonomy, disparate organizations can find some common ground through which their collections are categorized.

The medical industry also offers some standardized taxonomies that are shared across institutions. This enables physicians conducting research across different databases to be more productive, because they don't need to learn new taxonomies for each system.

Controlled vocabularies are lists of allowable terms that can be added to individual metadata fields. When compared to a taxonomy assignment, which applies to an asset as a whole, controlled vocabularies offer metadata consistency and standardization on a per-field basis.

Recalling our vehicle taxonomy example, an assignment to the *Rolls Royce* subject says something about the entire asset, but that doesn't help metadata editors maintain uniformity over the values in individual fields.

For example, say we had a metadata field that was intended to describe the state of the car in the photo. The terms we *expect* to see would be:

- In Motion (the car is moving)
- Still (the car is parked)
- Undetermined (state of car cannot be determined)

By presenting the metadata editor with a selection of allowable terms for this field, we ensure that all terms therein will be one of these three. Otherwise, our metadata would be polluted with terms like, "going" or "parked." When DAM users see the same list of allowable terms metadata editors saw (and used), finding things in the DAM becomes much easier.

Let's look at a few more examples we could use for other metadata fields.

Controlled vocabulary for describing the scene:

- Indoors (the shot was taken indoors)
- Outdoors (the shot was taken outdoors)
- Artificial (the shot has a computer generated or other unnatural background)

Controlled vocabulary for describing the perspective of the photo:

- Front Quarter (shot shows front and one side)
- Rear Quarter (shot shows rear and one side)
- Front Straight (shot shows front only)
- Rear Straight (shot shows rear only)
- Side Straight (shot shows side only)
- Top Straight (shot shows top only)
- Above (shot taken from above the car's horizon line)
- Below (shot taken from the below the car's horizon line)
- Other (shot taken from another perspective)

I've seen organizations try to integrate controlled vocabulary terms into their taxonomies, but they ended up with taxonomies that were so massive and detailed that virtually no one could use them.

Let taxonomies handle the asset categorization, while controlled vocabularies add the per-field metadata details.

Depending on your DAM's configuration, users will be able to assign a single vocabulary term to a field, or they'll be able to choose among several terms. Flexibility like this is key, because two or more terms can sometimes tell the entire story, or confuse it.

For example, a car in a photo is either *In Motion, Still* or *Undetermined.* (The latter can be the case when the photo is an extreme close-up of a car part, or an interior shot with no background.) The car cannot be two or more of those values—that makes no sense.

On the other hand, a *Front Straight* shot might be taken from *Above* or *Below* the car's horizon line. In this case, it would be useful to permit the assignment of more than one term. Granted, this would enable a careless user to erroneously assign *Front Straight* and *Rear Quarter*, which would make no sense, but you could opt for separate metadata fields for "Perspective" and "Level" if you wanted to stick to single-term assignments.

Another value in permitting users to choose multiple terms comes into play when the best choice is actually a cross between allowable options. For example, if you had a metadata field to describe the color of the car in the photo, you'd either have to have an impressive number of items in that controlled vocabulary, or you could let users build the best description from a reduced list of terms. For example, if the car is such a dark gray that it could be considered black, why not classify it as both?

When used together, taxonomies and controlled vocabularies help improve metadata consistency. This enables metadata editors to work faster, and it enables those searching for files to more quickly and easily find what they need.

Is a Rolls Royce a *car* or an *automobile*? Is it *expensive, costly* or *pricey*? Is it *British* or *English*? Don't let your DAM become a thesaurus. Offer some structure so that users won't have to guess what to think.

Freeform text fields are great for comments and other metadata values that are not expected to be the same across two or more assets. For everything else, design your DAM with consistency in mind.

Try to find some standardized taxonomies or controlled vocabularies for your profession. Google is a great place to start. For information and help specific to controlled vocabularies, I send people to ControlledVocabulary.com.

Whether you decide to use published taxonomies or controlled vocabularies or not, they can provide a wonderful learning experience with regard to how others have categorized the same sorts of digital assets you're likely to be using.

VAM, BAM, Thank You MAM

The Digital Asset Management industry has splintered into many ghettos over the years. You'll hear about Brand Asset Management (DAM does that), Media Asset Management (DAM does that), Marketing Asset Management (DAM does that), Video Asset Management (DAM does that), and scores more.

Digital Asset Management subclasses help vendors and analysts differentiate themselves (or confuse the market into thinking some meaningful differentiation exists), but you can forget about them.

I'll leave you in the capable hands of Google and Wikipedia to see if any of the alleged distinctions seem relevant to you. In the meantime, rest assured that everything you read in this book applies equally to all of it.

The Anatomy of DAM

It's not really important to fully understand the underpinnings of DAM technologies, but having at least a high-level understanding will help you cut through vendor marketing so you can better differentiate between what's important and what's smoke and mirrors.

Common to virtually all DAMs, the primary components of digital asset management software are:

- Database
- Permissions Engine
- Metadata Engine
- Search Engine
- Processing Engine

Database

The primary subsystem of any DAM is the database that stores the metadata. Most modern DAM systems use a database that's built on open standards, such as SQL, or that's an established player in larger enterprises, like Oracle. Some older DAM software is still based on proprietary databases the vendors built themselves.

DAM databases are collections of records, each usually representing one digital asset. So, if you have 2 million digital assets, you can at least expect to have 2 million database records. (Some DAMs use multiple records per asset, so this 1:1 correlation isn't always so.)

In turn, database records contain fields used to store metadata values, with each field representing one metadata value, such as a file name, due date or status. Metadata fields are presented to users via layouts. Some DAM systems offer a predetermined number of metadata fields, while others enable users to decide for themselves which metadata they'll need to track.

The most common type of metadata field is text. These fields, as the name suggests, are used to contain and edit text values, such as a contributor's name, keywords or comments.

Many DAMs also support other metadata types, such as numbers and dates. The benefit of fields specifically devoted to these data types is that they enable the DAM to more intelligently handle these values. For example, a user might want to find all assets whose licenses will expire in the next 30 days. Without some concept of how dates work, the DAM would have no idea how to perform the search. Likewise, if you're tracking the number of times an asset has been downloaded, you want to be able to generate reports that show those assets in some meaningful order. If the download numbers were stored as text, the DAM wouldn't have any way of determining the natural order of those values.

Another common metadata field type can store image data. This is what enables the DAM to store and display a thumbnail representation of the asset. It's also what more advanced systems use in order to be able to display multiple frames of a video, which makes it easier for users to get a sense of the video's contents, without having to watch it.

Other metadata types are available, too, but they're usually variations of those mentioned, or they're used for raw data storage by the DAM itself.

Permissions Engine

This is the part of the DAM that determines who can connect to the system, and what users can do once connected. Some systems provide a general set of access permissions, while others enable DAM administrators to determine with granular precision what each user can do, and when.

On a more basic DAM, you might have accounts for Editor, Designer and Everyone. Users would then share the account most applicable to their needs. Simplicity like this makes DAM management a breeze, but it also seriously limits the DAM's potential.

DAMs that offer more granular permissions enable you to define any number of users and groups, and then determine exactly what the members of each group can do. This is how, for example, you could use a single DAM to store the digital assets of several customers, while ensuring that one customer never sees the assets of another.

Flexibility and complexity travel as a team in the DAM world. That is, while a more granular system might seem desirable, mastering a complex permissions model takes more time, patience and testing. This isn't to say that all granular permissions models are so poorly designed that configuring them is impossible, but I have seen many customers of more "flexible" DAMs throw in the towel in disgust over the song and dance required to make the system usable.

Further, a more complex model can actually lead to weakened security if the person managing your DAM doesn't thoroughly understand how those permissions work. One of the most powerful features I've seen to address this enables a DAM manager or administrator to impersonate another user. In other words, the manager can temporarily assume all permissions granted to that user, which enables them to verify that things are properly (and safely) configured for that user. This functionality is also a godsend when you're trying to debug an access problem a user reports. If you go for a DAM with a more granular permissions model, make sure a feature like this is available. It will save you and your users much frustration.

Metadata Engine

When you add a new file to your DAM, a new database record is created and preloaded with some metadata. These initial metadata values come from the operating system and from each of the files added. The part of your DAM you can thank for the ability to extract metadata is called the *metadata engine.*

Metadata values generated by the operating system include file creation date and file modification date, file format and file size, and file location. These generic metadata values are applicable to all files stored on your computer, not just those you consider to be digital assets.

You can see some of these operating system-provided metadata values by viewing a file's Properties or Info window from your operating system desktop.

DAMs can also extract metadata values that are file format-specific. These values are embedded by the applications that created or edited the files. Examples include the number of pages in a word processing document, the names of fonts used in a layout, or the length of a video or audio clip.

Virtually all DAM systems can extract at least some operating system-provided metadata, because that's easy. Less easy is extracting these format-specific metadata values. There's no one DAM system that supports format-specific metadata extraction from all file types.

When you hear DAM vendors claim to offer support for any or all file formats, they're talking about operating system metadata. When it comes to the particular file types you use, it's important that you specifically ask the following:

- What metadata can your DAM extract from this file type?
- What editing options will I have for that metadata once it's inside the DAM?
- Can metadata values edited inside the DAM be written back into the associated file so that those values remain with the file when it leaves my DAM? (Think copyright, usage restrictions, license expiration and license renewal info.)

That last point won't be possible with a large number of files (and DAM systems), so make sure you completely understand the limitations of every DAM you consider.

Search Engine

DAM system capabilities vary wildly when it comes to searching. This is an area that's important to consider carefully. The most carefully edited metadata values do you no good if users can't use them to quickly find what they need.

Text-match searching is provided by virtually all DAMs. Using this technology, you type a search term or phrase, and the DAM system displays all records that include metadata values that match the search term. Some DAMs will try to find a match on any metadata field, while others enable (or require) users to choose which metadata fields should be compared for the search.

Text-match searching is popular, but it's not always the best option. For example, if you mistype your search term, you might not find what you expect. Google is smart enough to help with spelling and typos, but DAM systems are not Google.

Some DAM systems also enable you to find files by browsing categories or folders to which assets have been assigned. This search method is a lot like finding files by browsing through folders on your computer.

Though arguably the easiest search method available because it requires no typing or knowledge of existing metadata values, category browsing can be an inefficient means for finding files in larger collections. The reason for this is that some DAMs have extremely large category hierarchies. I can recall one specific installation that contained more than 16,000(!) different categories, some nested many, many levels deep. Navigating that system via category browsing could make one feel like a mouse in a maze.

Some DAM systems enable you to find images by making comparisons between images. Think, "find more like this."

Say you have one photo of the Eiffel Tower and you want to find other Eiffel Tower photos. Using the image you have as a goal, the DAM tries to find other images that show a similar pattern, presumed to be the Eiffel Tower.

This type of "pattern-match" searching doesn't always work as expected, so I find it mainly useful as a starting point. For a funny example of this technology breaking down, I once saw a photo of the Eiffel Tower return a photo of a saltshaker. In fairness, the two images *did* look very similar in silhouette. Again, it's a great place to start.

Another popular and useful search technology enables users to find (or reject) assets based on color palette matching. For example, if you were looking for a cover image to use on a UPS brochure, you might want to omit images saturated with the purple and orange that symbolizes FedEx.

This type of image search is less prone to errors than pattern-match searching, because comparisons are based on an image's color content, which requires no semantic understanding of the asset's actual content. For example, a photo of the ocean, when used as the target, might find photos of the sky, simply because both images contained high percentage of blue. Conversely, a photo of the sky or a sea scene could be virtually useless for pattern-match searching, if those images contain no discernible patterns.

Shopping sites like Amazon have popularized *faceted searching.* This technology enables users to define parameters that filter the search results they see. For example, you might choose a favorite brand and a specific price range. With this filter in place, you'd only see products that come from the company you selected, and that fall within the price range you defined.

This type of search is extremely useful, even if you're not selling products. For example, a DAM user searching for a brochure might want to limit the files she sees to only those in PDF format. This way, she won't have to sift through the layouts and images used within those brochures, many of which will share categories and keywords with the final PDF.

What's more, DAM managers might want to use faceted searching to limit what users see. This is a great way to make sure media releases aren't seen by the public until an embargo expires, and it can ensure layout artists don't see images that aren't yet approved for use.

Federated searching enables users to see results from many different databases, based on a single search. (Don't confuse this with a DAM being able to search across several of its own databases. This is easy and far less interesting.)

Google's shopping and flight-booking services offer nice examples of federated search. Using those services, the search info you enter pulls results from a number of systems, all in a single step. It seems so simple to those of us using these services, but what's going on in the background is really nothing short of amazing.

Federated search also offers tremendous potential for DAM, but without some standard agreed upon by DAM vendors, we're not likely to see such a thing become a DAM industry norm. Still, imagine how wonderful it would be to search for "Monet" in one DAM, and then see records from all museums in the world whose collections contain one of the artist's works.

Though this sounds similar in concept to what Google's Web search does now, the distinction is relevant. Google primarily searches the *content* of *static* files—it doesn't perform live database queries. The question is, of course, whether Google will ever see the content of the world's DAM systems as being anything useful to the majority of the world's Web users. Probably not.

Asset Processing Engine

Some DAM systems provide asset processing functionality. Asset processing refers to manipulating an existing asset in some way. This is what makes it possible for users to download Web- or email-ready versions of high-resolution Photoshop files, or post a segment of a DAM-managed video directly to YouTube.

The most common processing options include color space conversions (color to grayscale, RGB to CMYK), format conversions (EPS to PNG, Word to PDF), and cropping and scaling. More capable (and expensive) DAM systems can also perform video processing and even transcribe voice audio to text.

The functionality you need will obviously depend on how you plan to use your DAM. For example, if your organization uses, or plans to use, lots of video, make sure the system you choose enables users to do things like choose a thumbnail for the video, define ranges of frames that can be played back over the Web or, as mentioned, upload the video, all or in part, to YouTube or another video service.

Built-in asset processing seems wonderful on the surface, but make sure you test the results of every system you consider. Some DAM systems use primitive processing modules that don't yield acceptable results. Though you might be able to extend the system's capability through plug-ins, you must factor this into your cost and complexity equations.

Again, asset processing is not a trivial matter. Make sure you *thoroughly test* the capabilities of any DAM you consider. You're more likely to be disappointed than impressed. Make sure your expectations and needs can be met.

As a rule, it's probably best if the DAM doesn't rely on any internal, proprietary asset processing engines. No DAM vendor is as adept at asset processing as companies that are dedicated to the function. Further, today's processing needs will be child's play in a few years. You'll want to be able to hook into the most recent advancements in asset processing, and those are highly unlikely to come from a DAM vendor.

File Management Engine

It's not unreasonable to assume you'll be able to perform (at least) basic file management tasks from your DAM. After all, as we know now, files are the containers that house digital assets. They must, therefore, be managed.

Among the features users expect most are "smart" backups that consider file edits or other attributes, file renaming that can be based on rules or automation, and checksums that ensure file integrity. These features, however, are surprisingly absent from a number of DAMs. Instead, vendors ask users to rely on other software to protect their files.

This has never made any sense to me. Once a DAM is in place, I reckon it should be the only place anyone—administrator or user—should ever have to go to when working with files.

I'm *almost* willing to grant an exception to this rule to vendors that offer SaaS systems. In theory, Cloud-based systems backup original files just by uploading them into the DAM. But for DAM systems that index files in place on file servers, there's no excuse.

But this illustrates an important point: Take nothing for granted when considering a DAM. Make absolutely certain that what you need is available in any DAM you consider. A number of these functions can certainly be handled by external software, but what's the point of a centralized DAM system that requires external software for even the most basic functions?

Why You Might Not Even Need DAM

DAM appears on the must-have lists of more organizations each year. People speak of the need for DAM like they speak of the need to "go green." It's like unless the whole world climbs aboard the Digital Asset Express, global calamity is assured.

There's no question that DAM can offer benefits, but it's fair to admit that the sudden euphoria behind this 20-year overnight sensation is largely attributable to a passionate industry of DAM vendors, analysts, bloggers and conference producers. Phrases like "the proliferation of digital information" and "the need for workflow automation" have spooked would-be DAM users into thinking they've already fallen behind the curve. Without DAM, we're warned, all our data will one day disappear, our careers following soon thereafter.

But is it true? If you don't "DAM up" right away, should you start "making arrangements" for your digital assets?

I don't think so.

If DAM functionality was truly so critical to everyday computing, we computer users would have long ago demanded operating system features to enable us to identify, manage, find and use our files. We would have likewise insisted on hierarchical structures we could use for organization. In fact, we wouldn't have stopped making demands until we had all that *plus* some way of easily copying data between locations for backup and archival purposes.

Well, I don't know what's going on inside *your* computer, but I get all of this functionality from my operating system today—and I didn't need to start an "Occupy OS" movement to get it.

When I create new files on my computer, I can name them, rename them, place them into any folder hierarchies I need, find them using built-in search tools, and I can even add keyword tags to describe their contents. To ensure I don't lose those files, I can easily copy them to external hard drives, or even Cloud-based services. For under $50, I was even able to buy a little software program that manages all my backups automatically.

If this isn't "digital asset management," it sure smells like it to me. What's more, the vast majority of the world's data is managed exactly this way— using the tools of the OS, without a DAM in sight.

If you think your organization is the last on earth to see the light of DAM, you can relax. In fact, you could hold off on implementing DAM for another year or more and you'd *still* be ahead of the game.

Further, the need for DAM is not inevitable for all organizations, in contrast to what the DAM industry would have you believe. DAM is a lot like medicine for erectile dysfunction—when it's needed, it will be obvious to everyone involved.

The reason organizations can keep things under control without DAM can be attributed to Microsoft, Apple, Google and the Linux developer community. As DAM evolved, so evolved the operating systems we use.

For example, the Macintosh Finder had no "find" feature when it was first released. It would have been more aptly named the Macintosh Browser. Windows Explorer, on the other hand, was appropriately named when first released, because using it to find anything was nothing short of an exploration—pack a lunch, and don't forget the sunblock.

Since computing's Dark Days, however, a few important things have changed:

1. Operating systems have become much more sophisticated.
2. We users of those operating systems have become much more sophisticated.

Setting aside that first point for a moment, consider the second. We have learned to adapt pretty well to the limitations of our operating systems.

Supporting this theory are the ever-exhausting computer platform wars. On our computers, we have Windows, Mac and Linux. On our phones, we find Android, BlackBerry OS and iOS. We debate which is best when, in reality, they're all a mess. We have learned, however, to adapt to their weaknesses so well and completely that we actually start to *like* them.

Working within the constraints of these imperfect tools, we've learned to establish file naming conventions that convey meaning, and we've built complex folder structures that reflect business processes.

We've even defined workflow policies that enable us to effectively move files through these messy environments. You know the drill: you add your initials to the names of files you've approved; you move completed files into a certain folder; and you never send out any file without asking Nancy if it's ready to go—no one would ever even *think* of it.

By the end of a project, we have "Media Release – Final.pdf," "Media Release – Final 2.pdf," and the obligatory "Media Release – Final (Needs Review).pdf."

Only Nancy knows which version is the right version. May God bless Nancy and keep her forever in good health.

However error prone and tedious these practices are, they nonetheless qualify as digital asset management in the sense that we are managing digital assets.

Users have, in fact, become so good at overcoming operating system limitations that it's become tougher for DAM vendors to sell their wares. Twenty years ago, for example, DAM could be sold on the simple promise of making files easier to find and use.

In those days, digital images were represented by generic icons that offered no pictorial representation of a file's content; file sharing required floppy discs, computers using the same OS, and a gigantic leap of faith; and *finding* files was accomplished only by *browsing* through files.

By introducing such now-routine features as thumbnail images, cross-platform networking, and metadata searching, DAM vendors could clearly demonstrate the value their systems offered versus the OS. Customers lined up, check books open, and the fledgling DAM industry was born.

Let's now go back to that first point, the increasing sophistication of computer operating systems. If you see a generic icon on your desktop today, you probably think something has gone wrong. We virtually always see icons that offer some assistance with regard to what's inside the file. Further, if you search and don't find what you expect, you might even get cranky. And when was the last time anyone was concerned whether a Mac user would be able to open a file created on a Windows machine?

We expect much more from computers today, because operating systems have evolved. Homegrown digital asset management workflows have been built based on what OSes can do today. And you know what? Those workflows work pretty well, most of the time, for most organizations.

So why, then, would I write this book? And why should you care to read it?

The practices we've honed for OS-based digital asset management don't scale well. The more projects and users that are involved, the more difficult it becomes to mimic DAM functionality using an operating system.

When managing only a handful of projects, it's pretty easy to keep files organized. It's also easy to communicate file locations and change requests to others working on those files. But when you have 20 or more projects in development at any given time, and you have 5 or more project managers (each with his or her own way of doing things), OS-based DAM becomes extremely error prone.

This is this point at which many DAM converts first realized the OS lacks one very important feature required for effective digital asset management on a larger scale: policy and process definition.

When managing 20 projects on your operating system, it's up to *you* to enforce your established workflow rules and best practices. *You* need to explain to users where to store files that are ready for review, and *you* need to notify reviewers when those files are ready. Of course, you also need to send reminders when things are overdue.

Forget any of these steps and the workflow breaks down. This is when DAM can become your best friend. This is exactly the sort of thing a good, properly configured DAM can do for you, 24 hours a day, 7 days a week.

If things are going well at your organization right now, and you don't anticipate this changing any time soon, don't let the DAM industry intimidate you into thinking you need a change. Change isn't *always* a good thing when it comes to production pipelines.

Likewise, DAM isn't always a good thing—particularly if you saddle yourself with horrible DAM software, or kill the potential of good software through misconfiguration. Some DAM software is such a disaster, in fact, it's a wonder the Red Cross doesn't offer technical support.

On the other hand, if the limitations of OS-based DAM are starting to slow you down, or introduce errors into your production pipelines, a good DAM could be exactly what you need.

DAM Initiative Planning

Once you're (at least mostly) certain DAM is for you, the next step is to start planning your DAM initiative. That's right, *initiative*. Digital asset management is about much more than software.

In fact, software is among the least important aspects of DAM to consider—at first. You certainly don't want to saddle yourself with DAM software that can't do what you need, but avoiding a disaster like that will become much easier once you better understand what you'll need from DAM.

DAM initiative planning will help.

Gather Your Team

DAM works best when it's integrated into the business processes it will affect, meaning those processes rely on the contribution DAM makes. To better your chances of making this happen, it's important to build a team of people at your organization who are willing to share the burden and responsibility of your DAM initiative's success.

Depending on the size and complexity of your organization, your DAM team might consist of a handful of people, or it might be a roomful. At the very least, make sure you have the following bases covered:

DAM initiative owner – This is the person ultimately responsible for the initiative's success. This book assumes that's you.

DAM software manager – This person will serve as the go-to person for DAM software-related issues and questions: "How do I connect to our DAM from my Android tablet?"

Technical representative – Most commonly from IT, this person should have an understanding of your organization's technical infrastructure, and also have the authority to make decisions with regard to computer and network systems: "Can you please do what's needed for our DAM to use our LDAP system for authentication?"

Librarian/archivist – Though too many organizations forgo such a position, a person who has experience with collections management can be a godsend when it comes to ensuring your DAM initiative covers all the bases, and that your DAM software is well configured for usability: "Should we be organizing assets based on client name or year?" You'll later read more about the benefits these professionals provide.

Key department representatives – These people will represent the needs of the departments who will be the primary users of DAM at your organization: "What problems are users in Legal facing these days when it comes to finding documents?"

It's possible for a single person to serve multiple roles, but always try to involve the person at your organization most qualified. Resist the urge to not involve people because you want to keep the team small. Expertise is always needed, and political battles will take down a DAM initiative faster than anything.

For example, if you decide to handle technical issues yourself instead of involving IT, this will not serve you well in the long run. At some point, IT involvement *will* be required. IT professionals can often be more willing to offer advice than rescue. I was once told by an IT person, "Your failure to properly plan should not become my emergency."

Involve IT now, before your initiative's survival depends on it. If you find no one in IT interested or willing, try harder. If you still have no luck, you might just thank them for their consideration, and then ask them individual questions, as needed. The notion of "involvement" might sound like a commitment, whereas individual questions might be tolerable.

It also never hurts to respond to their answers with, "I really appreciate how willing you are to help! We're so lucky to have you!"

Likewise, don't fail to involve representatives from other stakeholder departments. If your DAM is intended to serve the needs of Marketing, and no one from Marketing is part of the team, trouble is inevitable.

Have I mention the politics upon which successful DAM initiatives are built and sustained?

In addition to diversifying and increasing available expertise, your DAM team (should) enable you to delegate responsibilities. For example, just as you're putting the finishing touches on your DAM software configuration, someone will need to be coordinating users to test the system, and collect feedback. Once deployed, while you're dealing with bugs and configuration issues, someone will have to be getting the word out and training new users.

DAM is just not something you want to try to do solo. Chances are, this isn't your only responsibility at work. Share the load; don't make yourself crazy.

Here are some pointers for putting together "Team DAM":

Draft a high-level plan – Though you can't at this stage be expected to know exactly *how* your initiative will solve your organization's problems, you can certainly draft a simple document that reminds others of the problems you aim to solve. Initially, this will serve as the "sales letter" you offer those you want to join the team. But the document will offer ongoing value, because you'll often have to bring new people up to speed on why you're doing what you're doing.

Find a partner-in-crime – If you can get another person on board before you ask others at your organization to join the team, you'll be in a better position. When *two* people are behind a seemingly implausible idea, the idea seems less implausible. Increase your credibility and divide your workload by finding a best friend fast.

Test interest – Before you identify your team targets, have a few casual conversations to see who might also be thinking a DAM (or similar) solution is needed. In doing so, you'll also get a better feel for who thinks everything is perfect as it is, and that no change is needed. Probably best to not recruit these people.

Avoid mass emails – Once you're ready to ask (beg) for help from others, avoid sending a generic email addressed to too many recipients. "Please respond" emails sent to multiple people can be as effective as emails sent to no one. Everyone waits for someone else to respond first. And once that happens, the others think, *Okay, that's covered—nothing for me to do now.* If no one responds, everyone thinks, *Well, at least I'm not the only one ignoring this.* I've been more successful sending the same content to recipients one at a time. When people think an email was meant for them personally, they feel more obligated to reply.

That last point can be a great ice-breaker for sparking up conversations with your marketing people. Ask their opinions on the topic and, no matter what response you get, follow up with, "That's amazing! Insight like yours would be such a great help to me on this project!"

Seriously, putting together a DAM initiative can be like campaigning for office. This just isn't the time for you to try to maintain your honor or dignity. Grovel, if it will help you build a great team. Ultimately, you'll leave your organization in a better place than you found it, and all the groveling will have been worth it.

Buy-in

One of the most valuable and immediate benefits your DAM team can offer is to help you secure the buy-in you'll need from others. Buy-in is important—particularly when it comes from executive offices—because things sometimes go wrong. And when they do, you'll need that support to get your over the humps. Examples include:

Cost – DAM initiatives aren't cheap, even if your DAM software is. When you factor in the staff time for DAM management and training, and you consider things like storage space, costs can add up fast.

Change – No matter how bad things are now, people are resistant to change. So when you approach your organization with your great DAM idea, there will be those who just won't have the patience for an organization-wide process change, even if they do see the benefit.

Setbacks – When things go wrong, even if only temporarily, naysayers find themselves with audiences willing to listen. You'll have enough to do trying to make things right; the last thing you need is to worry about public relations damage control.

If you can get the buy-in of Senior Management, your DAM initiative will stand a much greater chance of success. DAM is typically organizational in scope, so a directive from the top can be all the motivation that's needed to silences the naysayers.

Always put a senior face on your initiative, if possible. If you succeed, you not only have that authority behind your plan, but you have someone on board who won't want to be associated with a failed initiative. So, the pressure might increase for you from time to time, but the extra resources you need might be easier to find too.

The best way to get buy-in at any level is to be able to convincingly explain to others the benefits DAM will offer your organization.

This can be difficult, of course, because at this point in your initiative planning, you might be unclear about exactly what those benefits will be. Just do your best to match the problems your organization faces with the solutions you imagine are possible, based on what you read in this book and learn from other sources.

One tactic would be to take the high-level plan you created before you assembled your DAM team and expand it to include the input and perspective of your new team members. Add their names as authors, and turn that into your positioning document.

For example, let's say that one point made in your document reads:

"DAM will enable users to self-serve the files they need, without having to ask IT for help, and without having to ask for explicit permission to use each file."

With a little help from your team, that same point might be rewritten as:

"DAM will enable users to self-serve the files they need, without having to ask IT for help. IT estimates they spend approximately 20 hours per week helping designers locate and access files. This is half a full-time position that will be freed for more important tasks.

Further, DAM will ensure that the files our designers see have been properly licensed for use. Accounting says this benefit will not only save them time by making communication easier, it will help the company avoid costly litigation."

Speak in terms of tangible, measureable benefits and your arguments will sound more compelling. Speak in a voice that explains what *will* happen rather than suggests what *might* happen, and you'll sound more confident.

These tactics will increase your chances of obtaining the buy-in you need.

But it's important to remember that your credibility is at stake. Don't make promises based on the claims DAM vendors and their marketing materials make. It's unlikely you'll find a brochure that speaks to a product's limitations—and *all* products have limitations.

"Our new amphibious car can get from California to Hawaii faster than any boat!"

Sure it can, once you stuff it through the cargo door of a 747.

Always insist that DAM vendors show you *exactly* how everything works. Take no one's word for anything.

Find Some Experts

Before you get too far with your initiative, find someone you can trust to offer expert advice that's not rooted in any financial or product-aligned agenda. There's a lot to learn, and it helps to have someone on board who's done it all before.

Access to public community discussion forums is easy and free. In these forums, you're likely to find a searchable archive of many of the very same questions you'll think to ask. Further, you'll get connected with users who are already eyeball-deep in their own DAM initiatives.

LinkedIn has some DAM groups that consist of thousands of members. If you're not already involved, that's a great place to start. Make sure the groups you join are truly vendor-neutral. Some are sponsored by DAM vendors and, as such, tend to have many biased posts. It's not too difficult to see who's responsible for a group just by looking at the group manager, or the owner of any website associated with the group. Check that person's LinkedIn profile, or do some Web searching to see who's really in charge.

Many DAM vendors also host their own community forums. These can be great places to observe, because they can offer a good sense of community interest and satisfaction. If, for example, a vendor claims to have sold many thousands of DAM systems, yet the traffic in their user forum seems to come from the same 10 people over and over, this might be a red flag.

Another concern would be if most posts are about problems rather than ideas. Users who are enthusiastic about their software tend to offer ideas and best practice hints for the benefit of others.

Another thing to look for in vendor forums is participation from the company's employees. Do they care enough to involve themselves with their own community? If not, look elsewhere. Disinterest on the part of vendor employees is a systemic problem that will be apparent in far more than their user forum.

When you've exhausted the free resources, paid expertise is also available.

Some DAM vendors offer services departments they claim can help you with your purchase decision and everything else. They'll show you the ropes, help you determine your needs, enable you to choose the system that's best for you, and so on.

Should you be at all surprised if a vendor's software recommendation ends up being the very software they sell? Even if an individual employee's intentions are pure, vendor employees lack the bird's eye view you need to seriously consider all available options. They simply cannot know competing systems well enough to draw honest comparisons for you, even if they were so inclined.

You know what they say: When all you have is a hammer, all problems look like nails.

DAM industry analysts can also provide some help, but it's not cheap. Some analyst reports alone can cost thousands of dollars—and that's without paying for any human consultation or hand-holding.

If you're budgeting several hundred thousand dollars for your DAM initiative, analysts might offer some wonderful perspective and guidance. But I still recommend you do some research on your own before making any expensive expertise purchases.

Some of the analysts I've encountered didn't know enough about DAM to even be able to ask relevant questions. They would structure their research based on a very limited perspective, so it was actually easy to leave them thinking the system I represented was far better than it was.

For example, "Can your DAM ingest videos?" Yep. "So, would you say it's suitable for a video production company?" Yep. "Do you have many customers who use video today?" Yep. I saw my customers on YouTube all the time, so I knew they were using video in some capacity.

If I had been the analyst, I would have asked something more like: "Can your DAM ingest video? If so, please explain what a video production company would be able to do with the video they ingest using your DAM. Please describe that workflow in detail and then demonstrate it for me. Please also provide me with a list of video production companies willing to serve as references for your software."

But this was *not* what I was asked. I couldn't imagine what kind of advice these analysts were offering their clients.

Some analysts, on the other hand, not only knew exactly what to ask, they fully understood what I *wasn't* telling them, and they knew what that meant for their customers. When I would later see these analysts' reports, I made sure I commended them on a job well done.

Even though I was forced to promote the interests of a single vendor, I still wanted people to get all the information they could so they could make the right decision. I've seen what it's like when a prospect buys the wrong DAM. It's not pretty, and it made me sick when I felt like my work in marketing contributed to those bad choices.

Again, start out in those free forums and ask for advice. Ask about vendors, their software, their partners, best practices and everything else. Don't go further in your initiative until you're partnered with expertise you can trust.

Research and Interviews

In addition to your team and buy-in building, another major influence on the success of your initiative will be those who will use the system—your users.

I once heard a DAM manager joke that her initiative would be a huge success if it wasn't for her users. I laughed with her, but I really felt badly for her situation. She had done an exceptional job planning everything in her DAM initiative. But, she ultimately chose a DAM system her users found unusable.

You cannot overestimate the power and influence human psychology will have over your success. (So much so, in fact, I've devoted an entire section of this book to it.) If your initiative is hindered or derailed because your users end up disliking the system you provide, recovery will be extremely difficult. It's not easy to switch DAM software once you're locked in by contract or workflow investment.

No other aspect of your initiative is more important than user satisfaction. The best route to user satisfaction comes from understanding users, and the best route to understanding users comes from interviewing users.

The sooner you conduct your user interviews the better. Virtually every decision you make for your initiative will be influenced by the needs of users, so if you delay this important step, you might find yourself heading down some bad paths.

In addition to helping you get the information you need, interviews can turn your initiative's future users into allies today. People appreciate being asked their opinions. And when they find someone willing to listen to their pains, they're more likely to appreciate and grow to trust that person.

Interviews are also a great way for you to determine which users might be suitable for more responsibility within the initiative, and willing, of course. Anyone who has already been thinking about ways in which to improve the organization's digital asset woes could be a wonderful department representative, or even just a great sounding board for you.

If you don't know a lot about DAM when conducting your interviews, don't fret. These initial interviews should be about problem *identification*, not problem *solving*. That in mind, make sure to phrase your questions in ways that will encourage discussion and not biased or one-word replies.

For example, asking, "Can you think of any way that would enable you to get the approvals you need any faster?" will lead to a less biased reply than, "Would it help if approvers received emailed reminders when a review was due?"

The problem with "leading" questions like these is that they offer you, the interviewer, no meaningful information. When it's too easy for a subject to reply with yes or no, she will do so. Further, when your question poses a solution that seems reasonable, as did the example question above, you're inviting the user to simply agree.

Interview subjects using questions designed to get them to think, not just confirm the obvious.

Here are some examples:

Bad question: "Would it be helpful if our files were better organized?"

Problem: Who's going to say no to this question?

Good question: "If we were to better organize our files, how would this help you in your work?"

This question forces the subject to think, and it provides no bias that might influence the subject's response. You might hear about time savings, an ability to get more done, or a workflow less prone to errors. You might also hear, "That would depend on how they were organized." And this would be the start of your conversation on the topic.

Another example:

Bad question: "Do you need to access our files from home so you can work on your home computer?"

Problem: Whoa! Does this new DAM thing mean I'm going to have to start working from home too? In that case, no, I don't need to access files from home.

Good question: "Would you find it valuable to be able to do your work from locations other than your office?"

By rephrasing that question, you've suddenly got your subject thinking about that 4-day commute he's always dreamed about. And, you might be making a friend for your initiative, because your questions are starting to paint a picture of how this DAM thing could make things better for users.

This brings up a very important point: Users won't respond to what's better for the organization. People respond better to "what's in it for me" sales discussions, and make no mistake: User interviews are sales discussions. In marketing, we call it "needs assessment."

Having an idea of the questions you'll ask is good, but also important is how you'll handle follow-ups to the answers you receive. Interviewing is one part conversation and another part investigation—don't script yourself too tightly. Really listen to the responses you get, and ask follow-up questions relevant to those answers.

Here's a fictitious example of how badly a scripted interview can go:

Interviewer: Thank you for joining us, Dr. Ranger. Our readers are interested in learning more about your celebrated treatments for increasing mobility in younger adults who have suffered strokes.

Dr. Ranger: Our results have been astonishing! While we saw a marked 30% improvement in mobility over a two month period, we stumbled on something completely unexpected: That same stroke treatment, when administered to older adults, appears to cure all known forms of cancer!

Interviewer: So why, Doctor, do you think younger adults are having strokes today? Is it about lack of exercise, or bad diet?

Wrong! What started out as an interview about stroke treatments just became something much bigger. If you stick too closely to your script when your subject throws you a curveball, you'll miss the real story.

In addition, don't just take at face value the responses you get. Think about what subjects are *trying* to say. Some people don't always know the best ways in which to express their needs. Others have trouble recognizing when something is a problem.

For example, if a salesperson tells you she could get more work done if she could work while on the road, find out exactly what she means. If you instead note that "subject needs remote access," you might be missing the real point.

A follow-up question might reveal that when she travels, she doesn't take her laptop; she takes her Android tablet. Now you know that "if I could work while on the road" has as much to do with mobile platform access as it does remote network access. You could then reasonably assume users of iOS (iPhone/iPad) will request access too.

A layout artist might complain, "I waste too much time figuring out which files I can use in layouts." What does this mean? Is there no easy way to determine which files are approved for use, or does he mean that those responsible for granting those approvals hold things up?

Don't discourage ideas and input, no matter how off-base some responses might seem. Seemingly absurd suggestions can start making sense after others have filled in some of the blanks.

In summary, here are some points to remember when interviewing users about their digital asset management needs:

- Phrase questions so that subjects cannot respond with yes/no answers.
- Don't pose solutions in your questions—make subjects think for themselves.
- Listen to the responses you get and follow up appropriately. Remember, you're not trying to fill out a form; you're trying to learn what people need. Forget the script!
- Read between the lines to try to better understand what subjects are saying. Don't feel shy about admitting when you don't understand something you've been told. Phrases like, "help me better understand" can go a long way.
- Restate your understanding of what the subject has said. "Let me see if I understand what you're telling me…" This not only ensures you did understand it, but it enables subjects to hear their thoughts read back, which might prompt clarification or additional ideas on their part.

Once you've had a chance to digest all this information, pay attention to what you've learned. What you initially assumed was a need for DAM might prove to be something bigger. DAM might not even begin to address your organization's real problems, and the introduction of something entirely new could even make things worse.

Move forward with your initiative only if you think there's a reasonable chance that DAM can make things better. Otherwise, there's no reasonable chance for success.

Determine the Scope of Your DAM

There are two basic uses for DAM: file archiving and the management of works-in-production (WIP). It's important to keep a clear idea of which use is most important for your organization, because many of the decisions you make for your initiative will be based on this scope.

The distinction between the two comes from the state of the files being managed.

When used as an archive, a DAM manages files for which no further edits or modifications are expected. This is the most common use for DAM, and it's the easiest to set up, manage and use. Virtually all DAMs are capable of archive management.

Some DAM software can also be used to manage files still in development, or works in production. The additional functionality required to manage WIP includes handling edits, approvals, notifications and managing multiple versions of the same file.

If you need to manage works-in-production, be very careful about the DAM software you choose. The primary concern here has to do with the level to which the software can integrate into your organization's existing workflows. Content creators and editors don't like to go outside their creative environments to get and store files. If DAM services don't really make things better than they are, users will figure out ways around using the DAM, defeating its purpose entirely.

Users are far more tolerant when it comes to working with archive systems. It seems tolerable to visit an archive to collect what's needed, and then take it back into familiar creative environments for development. I suppose it's like visiting the market before making dinner: The intrusion is minimal and it can be scheduled into the workflow, making it an acceptable inconvenience.

The "acceptable" inconvenience of DAM visits can become insurmountable, however, for those eyeball-deep in asset development.

Creative applications become like walled gardens to those who use them. Once inside, users want to stay there for as long as possible, with minimal distraction. The last thing these artists want to do is repeatedly visit the DAM. For them, it's like being in the middle cooking a meal when you realize you have to run to the store for something you need.

To address the problem, some DAM vendors offer plug-ins and other tools that provide DAM-access right inside popular editing applications, like the Adobe Creative Suite or Microsoft Office. Users can find and place files, right from a palette that appears inside the creative application.

User-to-user communication and notifications are also required for WIP DAM. This is how users know when it's their turn to act on a file. Some systems enable users to send notes to another, while other systems take more charge over workflow, sending automated notifications.

Among the most popular requirements for WIP DAM is approval or review management. This feature enables users to send file links to reviewers, complete with review instructions. Reviewers can then see the files, make their suggestions, and approve or reject them, as needed. Any DAM that lacks this rudimentary feature shouldn't be considered a viable contender for WIP workflows.

If you plan to use your DAM system for works in progress, make sure you understand exactly how it will integrate into your existing workflows. Take nothing for granted, and accept no explanation without seeing and experiencing proof. I cannot stress this enough! WIP management is the most difficult thing for a DAM to do properly, and it's where you'll quickly see the shortcomings of some DAM software.

It's worth noting that any system that can handle works-in-production will most certainly also serve well as an archive. The one exception to this can come from search functionality. When DAM is to be used as an archive, search power and flexibility becomes even more important. So, while you'd be focused on workflow integration for a WIP DAM, stay focused on search capabilities when you're looking for an archive.

Also keep in mind that a WIP DAM system will require much more configuration and user training time. So, if you've planned and budgeted for an archive and then you decide it would be handy to also use the system for works-in-progress, be prepared for some significant revisions to your DAM initiative.

Integration with Other Systems

Providing asset and metadata services to other software systems in use at your organization can not only increase your DAM ROI, it can enhance the value you get from those other systems.

Through integrations, DAM files and/or metadata are made available to users of the integrated systems. Depending on the level (and quality) of the integration, those users might have no idea that all this information is coming from another system—the DAM.

While integration is a nice-to-have for some organizations, it can be the very reason DAM exists for others. When one thinks about the various business systems that could benefit from having access to a single, managed collection of digital assets, the value of integration becomes clear.

Here are some examples:

Customer Relationship Management (CRM) – Many CRM systems enable salespeople to send documents to prospects and customers. An integration between your DAM and CRM would ensure that when a document is sent, that document is always the most recent version, and that it was appropriate and approved for use.

Marketing Automation (MA) – These systems enable organizations to define unattended campaigns intended to nurture prospects through the sales cycle. A very over-simplified use case would be when a customer fills out a white paper download form on a website. The MA system enters the requester into the marketing database and then sends a thank-you email that contains the download links. If those downloads come directly from your DAM, you can manage versions from a single system, and track all those downloads along with your other digital assets. An integration between your DAM and MA would enable those working in the MA to choose files directly from the DAM for inclusion with their campaigns.

Product Information Management (PIM) – Organizations that manufacture products often have a central system that contains all product related information, such as descriptions, ID numbers and, of course, photographs. As valuable as these systems can be for internal information access and sharing, they become even more so when external retail channels can also leverage the information. Think about all those product photos you see on Amazon. Where do they come from? Who's making sure they're approved and up to date? An integration between DAM and PIM can help an organization ensure that retailers have the photos and captions they need. When updates are needed, the updates take place in the DAM and, depending on the integration, can be propagated throughout the retail network automatically.

Each of these systems could benefit from integration with a capable DAM, but imagine the DAM ROI that you'd get if your single DAM could speak to all your other business systems. Using only your DAM, you could update and approve all the photos, captions, datasheets and other information published across your entire enterprise and retail channel.

Without using DAM as a central repository for all these digital assets, each time a file or its metadata was updated, the new data would have to be manually propagated to each of those downstream systems. This could takes weeks and involve many individuals, and it's a workflow prone to errors.

If the idea of integration appeals to you (and I hope it does, because this is the future of DAM), there are a few things to consider as you move forward with your DAM initiative planning.

First off, do some Internet searching to see which, if any, DAM software has already been integrated with the other business systems you use.

If you find some options, try to find users or analysts familiar with the integration. Don't ever take for granted that a DAM vendor's advertised integration will work as you'd expect. (Or even *exists* at all.)

Technically speaking, "integration" means only that one system can send or otherwise make data available to another. This might be a long way from the peaceful coexistence you and your users envision.

Because of the "buzz worthiness" of the term integration, some DAM vendors announce integrations just to try to stay relevant. In fact, many of these integrations are half-baked, still in development, or just an idea they're floating to see if anyone's willing to pay for it.

Unless you see an integration working to your satisfaction, assume it doesn't. Be extremely skeptical here.

If you can't find any existing integrations that will suit your needs, all is not lost. Integrations are built on what's called an application programming interface (API). Don't choose a DAM that doesn't offer a published API—doing so will greatly limit your expansion options later.

Likewise, your other business software systems must offer APIs of their own. Assuming they do, communication between those systems and your DAM should be possible.

If a system doesn't offer an API, it might still be possible to build some sort of pseudo integration workflow based on non-real time metadata exporting and importing. In other words, at a given interval, your other system exports some data to a text file. Five minutes later, your DAM imports that data. Simple data exchange like this is really all you can hope for if either system lacks a functional API.

If you have on-staff software developers or other technical experts, tell them about your goals and ask about your options. Then, of course, ask if these folks would know how to build such an integration for you.

If your business systems do offer the APIs you need, but you have no one on staff to build the integration, do some Internet searching for "custom application development." Make sure you find a developer familiar with at least one of your systems—the DAM or the other system.

Integration can be an important factor in the success of your DAM initiative. When someone mentions the hottest new DAM software, and starts to tell you all about how it will change the world, politely interrupt and ask:

"Yes, but does it have an API?"

Defining Your Needs and Expectations

At this point in your initiative planning, it's time to take everything you've learned and define some goals you can use to populate a requirements document. Clearly defined goals can help you gain buy-in from bottom line-driven executives, and a requirements document that's built on those goals will help you communicate to DAM vendors and service providers precisely what you have in mind.

Speaking in terms of goals is important because this invites experts to figure out how to make it all happen for you. When you speak in terms of directives, you alleviate experts from having to add any value, or even save you from your own mistakes.

For example, say you're late for a flight. You jump into a cab and start barking turn-by-turn directions to the driver. Within minutes, you're stuck in an awful traffic jam. The driver mentions how he got stuck in the same mess on his way to your house. "Why didn't you tell me this was a bad route to take?" you shout. He replies, "You didn't tell me where you were trying to go; you just told me where you wanted me to turn."

Let your experts handle the details. Tell them only where you need to go, when you need to be there, and how much money you have to spend on the ride. Then, if what's delivered isn't what was ordered, you have a document that can clearly explain where and how the system delivered falls short.

Goals-focus is important when it comes to DAM selection because vendors interpret the meanings behind named features differently, and generously. If you define your needs by throwing around feature names, you give vendors wiggle room through which they can interpret your needs to align perfectly with their offerings.

"Your requirements document said you needed 'easy file sharing.' The system we delivered enables users to share files, and we think it's easy."

Instead of speaking in marketing terms that offer vendors wiggle room, stay focused on your goal. What do *you* need file sharing to do? How do *you* want file sharing to work?

The following paragraphs show how your requirements document can define "easy file sharing" in no uncertain terms.

"Authorized users must be able to choose one or more assets, choose one or more recipients, and then define a valid time period for the link. The sender should be able to define a date at which a download reminder will be sent to all recipients who have not already downloaded the file(s).

File sharing links should be sent via the sending user's standard email client and optionally uploaded to Google+, LinkedIn and Facebook in a single action. If logins are required, they must be handled by the DAM. Any recipients who have not downloaded one or more of the assets within the time defined by the sending user should be sent a reminder by the DAM that includes the download link. The content of reminders should be based on templates or configurations we can change at any time without IT or other technical assistance.

The sender should be able to choose one or more permitted download file formats for each included asset. These formats should be available from pre-configured options available in the system, and the sender should be able to configure custom formats that are available only for each shared link.

The sender should be able to select addresses from his or her standard email address book, or by selecting other known users of the DAM from a searchable list. Recipients should also be selectable from a list of Google+, LinkedIn and Facebook connections. The system should permit distribution lists to be saved, reused and shared with other DAM users.

Valid time periods should be definable based on specific date ranges, or by time periods that start upon initial download. In other words, when the recipient first clicks to download an asset, he or she then has x days during which the link will continue to function before it expires. All dates should be enterable via text or a calendar widget. The sender should be able to define the message shown to users who click on a link that has expired, or that is not yet valid.

The sender should be able to later change which files are included with the link so that the same link can be used for "What's New This Week" or other such ongoing uses. Each time the link is clicked, only those files currently selected for it should be made available.

The sender should be able to visit a dashboard that shows his or her shared links, with information about which recipients have downloaded which files. The sender should have the option to receive email notifications, sent at intervals he or she defines, that include report summaries of each link shared, and which recipients responded. Additional notification options should send an email the moment an asset from the link is downloaded. This notification should include the name of the recipient, the name of the file(s) downloaded, and the date and time of the download. All notifications should be bundled and sent at time intervals defined in the user's preferences, so that the volume of notifications sent can be managed."

Remember when we thought of this requirement as simply "easy file sharing"?

Trust me when I tell you that no DAM software on the market today contains all of the functionality described above. Yet, would-be DAM organizations expect much of this functionality to be standard on any DAM that claims to make file sharing easy.

By defining this requirement in terms of your goals and requirements, you leave it up the DAM vendors and service providers to prove to you they can address your needs. Or, they must detail exactly where they fall short.

And don't think you can't redefine your requirements and expectations at any time during your research. You'll certainly learn more as time goes on, so leverage that newfound knowledge. Who cares if you've already submitted a request for proposal (RFP) to a vendor?

Simply say, "by the way, I want more now than I mentioned in the RFP."

Define Policies (and honor them)

In my mind, the main difference between DAM software alone, and DAM software within a DAM initiative, is *policy*. DAM software is controlled by people; policy, in turn, is what guides those people.

Let's take a look at some of these policies.

Asset ownership – Once an asset has been created or acquired, your asset ownership policy will define who at your organization is responsible for that asset. If the asset needs an update, or if there's a licensing issue, the asset owner should be the go-to person to set things right again.

Asset ownership is policy best assigned to a position. In other words, don't define policy that states all photographs are to be owned by Chad; instead, say all photographs are owned by the Photography Manager. Today, that happens to be Chad, but tomorrow is another day. Further, when Chad leaves for his Hawaiian vacation, someone needs to assume his duties. When policy assigns photograph ownership to the Photography Manager, this gives you some flexibility with regard to accountability and system permissions configurations.

Initial indexing – This policy dictates when assets must be initially indexed (uploaded) into the DAM. If you're working with a work-in-progress (WIP) DAM, you might decide that all new digital assets must be cataloged within 24 hours of their creation, regardless of their current state of development.

For archive DAMs, you might decide that assets must be indexed once their associated project is completed. Your indexing policy should also define who's responsible for adding files to the DAM. Should it be the file creator? The project manager?

License renewals – If your organization licenses assets from others, you need policy that determines how many days before license expiration those assets should be evaluated for renewal.

The evaluation process should also be defined. Will it be based on use? Will an authorized user make the determination? Also decide what happens if an asset license will *not* be renewed. Should all projects that include the asset be marked for an update to remove the asset?

Local storage of assets – Some users will want to keep local copies of files on their computers, insisting this is more convenient always downloading fresh copies from the DAM. Will you permit this? If so, how will you control things like license expirations or updates?

This is a great example of how policy can dictate which DAM features you need. If you will permit users to store files locally, you'll need some way for the DAM to track who has local copies of each file. Some DAMs offer a "subscribe" feature that notifies users when things have changed.

Which files should be indexed? – This policy is important because not *every* file a user creates should be added to the DAM. Make sure you define what an asset is at your organization, and make sure all users understand that definition.

For example, what should Sales do when they receive a request for proposal? Should RFPs be indexed? Should they do so immediately, or wait until they have drafted a response, and then index the two documents together?

There are countless more such examples of policies that guide users, but you get the idea.

Now take a look at some of the ways in which a DAM can help you manage these and other policies.

Asset ownership – Your DAM can assign a user as the asset owner, based on rules you define. If you always make the indexing user the owner, that's easy. Or, if you define owners based on file type, that's easy too. But if *content* is what determines asset ownership at your organization, you need to think more creatively about this.

Using our previous example of photographs all being owned by the Photography Manager, how would the DAM know whether a given JPEG or TIF file is a photograph, as opposed to any other image? It could look for EXIF metadata, which would be like a fingerprint from a digital camera, but if the photo was scanned, this metadata might not exist.

You could also offer a menu to enable users to manually identify the content. This would work, but it would be time consuming if hundreds or more assets are indexed at once. Once that value was determined, however, your DAM could determine the correct asset owner based on the chosen value.

You might also define policy that states when Sam indexes files, they are handled as photographs, because that's all Sam deals with. Or, you could say that all newly indexed files must be reviewed by a manager before ownership is determined.

Initial indexing – If you need some DAM assistance to enforce your indexing policy, you can have the DAM automatically index new files it finds on users' computers. The ability to do this, of course, will depend on your organization's network and privacy rules, and the DAM you've chosen.

You might alternatively want to find a DAM that makes indexing particularly convenient for users, perhaps even reminding them daily with a list of all newly discovered files on their drives or network shares. Or, if you decide this responsibility is better left to employee managers, you could send the notifications to those people.

License renewals – Many of the rules you define for when or whether a license should be renewed can be handled by your DAM. That DAM can search for assets due for expiration in 90 or so days, and send that list to each asset's respective owner.

You might even configure those reports include the number of times the asset has been accessed in the past year (its popularity), or the number of projects in which it appears (how much update work would be required if the asset was taken offline).

Some DAMs will additionally be able to take expired assets offline, so they they're not erroneously used in new projects. Depending on the sophistication of your DAM, it might also be able to schedule update projects, and notify those who need to perform the updates.

Local storage of assets – No matter how much "Big Brother" you configure into your DAM, users will learn to outsmart it. So even if you have your DAM constantly searching local hard drives for file duplicates, users will get around this.

If you've defined policy that users find difficult to honor, perhaps a reevaluation of that policy is indicated. No good will come from forcing users to hinder their own productivity. Look into a DAM with subscription features or something similar that can help you manage the concerns of file duplicates, without alienating users.

Which file types should be indexed? – If you can define this policy in terms your DAM can understand, it should be easy enough to have the DAM disregard indexed files that don't meet your criteria for "asset." For example, if you don't want text or PowerPoint files indexed, the DAM can be configured to disregard files of these types. But if *some* PowerPoint files should be indexed while others shouldn't, you'll be at the mercy of user education and compliance, unless you can identify something unique about the "good" files that your DAM can recognize.

Policy definition is something you can start with right now, long before you start working with any DAM software. In fact, the sooner you start, the sooner you'll be able to create a requirements document that better reflects your needs. Remember, though, don't tell vendors and consultants how you want something to work; tell them the outcome you need.

Policy definition is also a great way to involve non-technical people from the various departments from which you'll eventually need buy-in. Policy is a discussion to which everyone can contribute, for whatever that's worth.

Hardware Matters Too

As significant as software is when it comes to the technical aspects of your DAM initiative, it isn't the only technological consideration that can affect the success of that initiative. While many of these considerations affect only those running DAM software on-premise, those running Cloud-based systems aren't entirely out of the woods.

This is where your IT ally will really start to earn his or her keep. Some of the topics you should discuss with IT are:

- Computer, if your software will be run on-premise (more on that later)
- Network access and limitations
- User account authentication
- Storage and backup space

Though the ultimate requirements of the computer you'll use for your DAM will be defined by the DAM software you'll be running, virtually all modern computer servers should be capable of running DAM software, at least for the purposes of testing. If you ultimately decide on an on-premise DAM, you'll want to make sure you have a computer well suited for your intended use. Again, speak to the DAM vendor and other users about realistic requirements.

Next, ask IT if they anticipate any issues with your DAM users connecting to the DAM via your organization's existing network.

This will be less of an issue if your chosen DAM software is on-premise and all the network traffic between users and your assets will be LAN-based. But if you've chosen a Cloud-based DAM, find out if any firewalls or other devices might hinder access. Speak to you DAM vendor to see if there are any special software tools required for DAM configuration. If these tools require nonstandard TCP/IP ports, IT will have to open these ports for you.

Also let IT know that your Internet access bandwidth requirements are expected to increase, perhaps substantially, if you choose a Cloud DAM. For example, if your organization's "pipe" to the Internet isn't that big, ongoing use of a Cloud-based DAM might noticeably degrade Internet performance for others at your organization if IT doesn't prioritize or otherwise manage that added traffic.

IT might have other questions with regard to the network "friendliness" of your DAM software. Your DAM vendor should be able to help.

User account authentication is a fancy way to refer to the process of making sure a user trying to connect to the DAM is a legitimate, recognized user. Virtually all DAM software will be able to handle user authentication natively, but some systems might also be able to offload this task to your organization's Active Directory, Open Directory or other LDAP (Lightweight Directory Access Protocol) authentication system. IT will know if such a system is in use, and your vendor will (should) know how to integrate that system with your DAM.

The advantage of authenticating users via LDAP is that you can use the same user accounts already configured in that system for your DAM. In other words, if you have 50 people in marketing who will each need access to your DAM, you won't need to create 50 new user accounts directly on the DAM system.

Some organizations consider LDAP integration to also offer a security benefit because IT can remotely disable access when an employee leaves. This is helpful to you, because you probably don't know all 50 of those marketing people. So when one leaves, it would be nice to know his DAM access is automatically disabled, even if you never knew the employee.

You'll also need to make sure you have ample centralized storage space for all your current and future digital assets. This won't be a hardware issue for IT if your system is Cloud-based, but that doesn't let you off the hook entirely. Some organizations have decided that even though they run DAM in the Cloud, they need to have local backups of their assets and metadata. See if IT agrees, and make sure your DAM vendor is willing to make that possible.

Plan Your Deployment

Once you've gathered your team, secured the buy-in you need, found some experts to help, determined the scope of your DAM and integration needs, identified your needs and expectations for the initiative, distilled your business processes and requirements into clearly defined policies, and made some decisions with regard to hardware and software, it's time to schedule and plan the launch of your DAM initiative.

Depending on the complexity of your initiative, you might be looking at months or even years before launch day. Evidencing the time required, the average sales cycle for DAM software is six months to two years—and that's just for the software alone! Doing DAM right takes time, and it's time you can't afford to skip.

Consider these important phases of DAM deployment, all of which must be completed or at least planned before you launch your initiative:

Research and requirements – This book has been, until this point, about *only* this phase. Expect this to take many months. You have interviews to schedule, research to conduct, requirements and expectations to define, and you have to do it all while you're learning. Rushing through this phase is the mistake most likely to saddle you with a DAM system that's not in line with your organization's needs or user expectations.

Project planning – Once you're completed your basic research and requirements assessment, it's time to get out a calendar and mark some milestones. This is also when you need to determine which resources will be available to you, financial and otherwise. Who will be your developers and testers, and when are they available? Will the documentation they'll need for testing be done on time? Is anyone scheduled to write that documentation? Will you be asking Management for money at the worst possible time of the year? Will you be launching at your organization's busiest time of the year, when no one will have time for the training they'll need to start using the system? The experts you befriend can be very helpful during this phase.

Development and/or configuration – This phase describes the actual software development and configuration you'll need to make your DAM software do what you need. Depending on your requirements and the DAM system you choose, this phase might last a few weeks, or it might last for years. Like everything else, the configurations you'll need will be based on—you guessed it—your requirements. Find a DAM that closely suits your needs and you'll spend less time in this stage. As a rule, think of customization as something you do to make the DAM better. If it's required to make the DAM usable, find another DAM.

Testing/QA – Like any good software developer (because that's what you've become), you need to plan a user testing and quality assurance (QA) process. This phase will consist of giving DAM access to your chosen testers, having a process in place for them to report their findings and concerns, and making sure all that feedback goes through your own approval filter before it reaches the developers who will squash the bugs and make the changes.

You'll also need an evaluation guide for your testers that will explain the basics of the system and offer a list of things you'd like them to test. Make sure you set aside *at least* a month for testing. Many problems will be found within a week or two, but you'll need time to fix them and restart the testing. (New builds can introduce new problems.) Further, users need time. They have other jobs to do, so testing your DAM will be something they do when they can.

Launch – If you've done all your planning and testing according to plan (and you've done a good job!), your actual launch will be somewhat anticlimactic. When a new software system is launched, only the computer's microprocessor knows—the real promotion is up to you.

Once the system is live in exactly the configuration actual users will first experience it, it doesn't hurt to go through a final round of testing before you move on to promoting the initiative.

Promotion – How you promote your system will depend largely on what options are available to you at your organization. It will also matter whether your users are entirely internal, or whether outside partners and customers will also make use of your DAM.

Email is a useful vehicle, but consider from whom the email should be sent. Something that comes from your CEO might get more attention than email that comes from you.

Fliers posted around the office or campus can help, and social media channels assaulted by your entire DAM team at once can help too.

Also consider advertising the system on your intranet or, if the DAM will be available to partners and customers too, add a link on your public website.

Most important, remember that repetition is key in advertising. Don't announce your initiative once. Make a plan that includes follow-up announcements for at least six months.

Training – As part of your initial announcement, offer training sessions and documentation. Whether the training is classroom based or virtual via webinar software, make sure it's convenient for users.

Don't offer just a single class; offer classes on different days and different times. If you'll be providing virtual training sessions, record them for playback by those who can't attend the live sessions. If your company, partners or customers speak more than your native language, try to offer trainings in all relevant languages.

It's important to keep in mind that your DAM will become so familiar to you that you might think it requires far less training than it does. But it's all new to your users, and they might not always be in the mood to learn something new. Good training is always part evangelism, so keep that in mind.

Support – Always make sure your users have access to the support they need, preferably before they need it.

Don't just offer download links to the user guide for your chosen DAM software and leave it at that. This is a recipe for misery, for your users and for you. The documentation you provide should explain *your* DAM software configuration through the lens of *your* DAM initiative, and it should always be freely available, and easy to access.

The amount of documentation you offer will depend on the complexity of your initiative and software. There's no need to completely rewrite your

DAM vendor's documentation, but users will at least expect a quick-start overview of what they need to know.

If writing isn't your thing, sit yourself down in front of your laptop or tablet camera and start making how-to videos. Keep them short, and jot down a rough script you can use to keep you focused.

Armed with the best proactive support you can offer, users will still have questions that are best answered by a human. One-stop shopping for all support needs will yield the best results. Don't expect users to know that Lisa handles technical issues, while Moesha manages content issues. The distinction between "technical" and "content" will blur for users, and they'll become frustrated.

When users seek support, something has already gone wrong. Users in distress are seeking a solution, not an education.

DAM Return on Investment (ROI)

If you need to (or just want to) calculate ROI for your DAM, you have your work cut out for you. This isn't to say that DAM, when properly planned and executed, can't save you money; it certainly can. But the metrics often used to calculate ROI for digital asset management can be, let's say, dubious.

Many DAM ROI examples you'll see involve putting a price on staff time, determining a time savings, and then multiplying those numbers to get a daily savings. That number is then multiplied into an annual savings that's so amazing that you'd figure a $50,000 DAM will pay for itself in a year, even if only a single person ever used it. Multiply that savings by the 500 people at your organization who will use your DAM, and you discover that your company will save $25,000,000 in the first year alone.

This is an absolutely amazing return on a $50,000 investment!

It's also absolutely fictitious.

Before I go further, let me say that if you're only interest in calculating DAM ROI is to appease some corporate mandate, and you think the formula above will work, then go for it. But I want to speak to what I perceive to be the reality of DAM ROI calculations, because I don't think we should believe our own DAM hype.

Here are the primary problems I have with this formula:

It's extremely difficult to estimate exactly how much time an individual user will save because of DAM: Users work at different paces and skill levels. So, when an individual DAM feature, like search, is to be paraded as a time saver, one must first consider the skills of the user.

For example, one user might claim she saves two hours a day finding what she needs in the DAM, while another user says he knows the organization's files so well that he can find anything he needs within moments, without the DAM.

Based on these two interviews, the ROI investigator adds "2" to the time savings of one user, while he adds "0" to the time savings of the other.

The problem is that the "fast" user should have been asked a very important follow-up question: "Does the DAM slow you down?" If so, that value should have been added as a time savings minus.

Power users often adapt so well to the "pain" their organization's feel, that their productivity can actually be hindered by the "solution" to that pain. If time lost isn't factored in to the time-savings metric, the metric will be flawed.

Additional tasks are required when DAM is in place: Indexing and tagging digital assets takes time. As important a practice as this is, it adds time to workflows. This is time that wasn't required before the DAM, so it needs to be factored in as another time loss against the time-savings metric.

Users don't always tell the truth: When a manager asks an employee if some new widget is saving that employee significant time, that employee can go into defense mode. If she says yes, she fears she'll be assigned extra tasks; if she says no, and the manager is pro-widget, she fears retribution.

When DAM automation features are in place, users might become downright fearful for their jobs. When staff savings start to add up, it doesn't take long until Management starts to reevaluate the need for all those positions. Users aren't stupid; they know this.

A manager might be able to counter skewed users perspectives by carefully accounting for employees on a per-project basis. But a creative production isn't a fast food counter, so this is pretty unlikely.

Even if your organization does calculate per-project time, that number is probably used for client billing. So do you want the number to be high for more profitable billing, or do you want it low to justify DAM ROI?

Workdays calculated don't account for time off: What amazes me most is when I see that daily savings calculated against 365 days in a year. It only *seems* like we work 365 days a year. In truth, between weekends, holidays, time off and sick leave, we work far fewer than 365 day each year.

Start-up and ongoing costs of the DAM are rarely considered: Sometimes I see a DAM ROI calculation that factors in varying costs and savings in the first-, second-, third-year and so on. When fairly determined, the first year typically shows no ROI because of DAM start-up costs.

Usually missing, though, are the ongoing costs of the DAM. The updates, the IT time, the computers, the meetings, the software maintenance contracts, all that recurring training for current employees, and all that startup training for new employees.

A DAM needs care and feeding, which takes time and money.

The real costs of not having DAM aren't considered, because no one knows them: An assessment of "what's wrong now" is an exercise few organizations undergo before looking into DAM. Do they know the cost of recreating lost files? Have they tracked how many times an asset was licensed twice because Department B didn't know that Department A had already purchased a site-wide license?

Most organizations have no idea about these and other costs. But without this data, it's not possible to credit the DAM for its part in avoiding these issues.

These and many other factors contribute to what makes me a DAM ROI skeptic. On occasion, I've seen examples of DAM providing indisputable ROI, but this is rare. In the vast majority of cases, managers and users tend to just have a sense about the value their DAM provides.

More importantly, while we're so focused on a return-on-investment, shouldn't we also be focused on a *return-on-creativity*? When you provide an environment in which creative geniuses can be more creative, the returns can be immeasurable.

Who cares about saving a designer an hour or so a day? What matters is doing everything you can to enable that designer to come up with the world's best ad campaign or logo. And you'll do that by not hindering him with poorly designed DAM software or poorly planned DAM initiatives.

In my opinion, this should be the goal of any DAM initiative. ROI will follow in time.

Staffing Considerations

No DAM initiative can function without adult supervision. Though a number of the positions required (or recommended) might be handled by those already on your DAM team, your organization might insist that you explicitly define staffing requirements before funding is granted. These recommendations can help you define those requirements.

Initiative Owner

Someone has to accept ultimate responsibility for your initiative. There will be decisions to make and questions to answer. If no one is in charge, your initiative will, in time, lose direction, and probably support too.

The owner must serve as the face of your system and one of its chief evangelists. This person should also possess, perhaps more than anything else, a high level of enthusiasm for (and understanding of) the initiative, its goals and its potential.

Ideally, the owner has at least some technical smarts to be able to understand the underlying technologies in play, and be able to appreciate the relevant differences between DAM software. This becomes additionally beneficial when things go wrong, because reparative actions won't be delayed while novices are scrambling to figure out what went wrong and whom to call for help.

Authority is always a plus for the person in this position—the more authority the better. DAM requires ongoing money and resources, so it's nice to be able to approve such things without too much fuss.

Think of your DAM initiative's owner as its CEO, CFO, CTO and CMO all rolled into one.

Systems Manager

This is the person responsible for the computers, network and software aspect of your initiative. Outside of this function, your system manager might have little if any involvement in the system. Most of the time, this function is managed by someone in IT. This works fine, so long as you have ready access to the help you need.

If your organization is large, and your DAM initiative will be well funded, a dedicated system manager can be tempting. I would hold off on that, though, because you might find you have better uses for that money. It's unlikely you'll have enough for this person to do once the DAM is up and running.

Your system manager should have a strong knowledge of your organization's IT infrastructure, and she should also have the authority to make decisions with regard to LAN and remote network access. A working knowledge of your DAM software would be ideal.

Librarian or Archivist (Information Professional)

This is the position that surprises people more than any other. Why, people wonder, would a *librarian* be needed with a *digital* asset management system?

And what's an archivist anyway?

Today's librarians don't fit their profession's stereotype. In fact, librarians have been on the fore of the digital data revolution for decades. But this isn't the main reason your initiative could benefit from the expertise of one of these information professionals.

DAM is all about organization. People can't use what they can't find. Archivists and librarians are professional organizers. Where you or I might stare at a collection of files and have no good idea how to categorize them in some way others will understand, informational professionals know exactly what to do, how to get started, how to document it all, and how to train people to make use of it.

Keep in mind, it was a librarian who created the Dewey Decimal system more than a century ago. And librarians have been using and improving that system ever since. Usable organization of diverse works is in their DNA.

Information professionals are also ideal for helping your organization determine appropriate taxonomies.

If you can't afford to staff an information professional full time, look for freelancers who offer this service. They can help get you up and running, and remain a resource you can contact whenever you need.

Technical Developer

Unless your needs are extremely simple, you'll need someone who can do the technical heavy lifting for you. This includes DAM system configuration to ensure things work as you need, and integration with other systems, including your website or anywhere else you plan to publish digital assets outside of your DAM software.

Don't confuse this position with your System Manager position. That position's interests lie solely with making the hardware and software work. A System Manager has little if anything to do with making your DAM work properly, or with making it work with other systems.

You might be able to outsource this position to a freelancer, the services team of your DAM vendor, or a third-party DAM services company. There are benefits to all three options, but trust no one to be able to do the job until you see and speak to references that impress you.

Don't assume your DAM vendor's professional services team will (or even can) provide the best service. I've seen examples of what happens when a vendor's internal services team lacks the skills and experience required to provide truly *professional* service to its customers.

Further, the interests of a DAM vendor's services team might be skewed. They might have add-ons and upgrades to sell, and sales quotas to meet. Worse, they're much less likely to admit when a problem is the result of a limitation, design flaw or bug in their own software.

A third party can offer an unbiased perspective that can help you make better decisions with regard to your DAM.

As you'll do when considering the DAM software, check into user communities to see which system integrators or vendor partners others recommend. (And don't forget to check those references!)

A good, reputable professional services team will have scores of customers willing to tell you about the great service they received. If references aren't offered, consider other options.

If you decide to make your Technical Developer a staff position, it's obviously best to find someone who already knows your DAM software and other business systems. But if you can't, don't make this a deal-breaker. If you find someone with extensive technical experience whom you suspect or know to be a solid performer, that person can likely acquire the expertise you need.

Many of the best DAM integrators I've seen had no previous DAM experience when they started. They did, however, come into their DAM positions with proven technical experience.

Focus on finding a good person who has the general technical and self-educational skills required to get the job done. It can also help if this individual has a creative streak and some enthusiasm for technical possibilities. A technical guru who's a fountain of fresh ideas can really help move things forward. People like this are not easy to find, but they're worth the effort.

By making an investment in a great Technical Developer, you not only gain someone who can make System A dance with System B, you'll have another technical watchdog on your team who can make sure you're always making good decisions, and that the DAM software you chose was, and continues to be, the right choice.

As the Cloud enables and encourages more and more systems integration, the value (and cost) of positions like this will dramatically increase. So start shopping now.

Database Manager

At this point, you've considered the person who will keep the machines running, the person who will help you define the best organizational methodologies, and the person who can tweak your DAM to do exactly what you need, and to speak to other systems.

Now, what in the DAM world is a *Database Manager*?

If you think about these other positions, they are global in scope. What these people do affects your *entire* DAM initiative. But each department in your organization will have requirements that are unique. They'll each want to manage different metadata values, and they'll each have different "local policies" that govern particular own use of the DAM.

This is where your Database Managers come in.

Each Database Manager will represent the interests of a given department within your organization. Each manager will ultimately determine what metadata fields his department requires, and what workflow considerations must be in place for his department.

Though Database Managers will work under the umbrella of your DAM initiative as a whole, they are accountable first to the departments they represent.

Marketing's interests, for example, will be all about distribution. They'll want files to be easy to access, and they'll want to easily provide new versions when typos are found, or when content needs to be updated.

Legal, on the other hand, insist that their documents remain absolutely secure, and that content that's been archived remains archived in *exactly* the state it was in when committed to the archive.

Both departments will want to see usage history, but for opposite reasons: Marketing will want to make sure more and more people are accessing their files, while Legal will consider usage reports to be an audit trail that shows exactly who has seen what.

In a former position, my marketing team referred to the person responsible for legal affairs as the Director of Sales Prevention. That's how different departments can be, which is why a representative from each department can really help keep the peace.

Database Managers should have the technical skills required to make changes to the portions of the DAM they manage. They should also have the ambassadorial skills required to liaise between the DAM team and their respective departments.

Consider this position part technical and part political, with a good sense of organization thrown in.

Metadata Editor

Metadata Editors are responsible for making sure all ingested assets are properly tagged and otherwise described via metadata. Improperly tagged assets are as good as invisible, so the holders of these positions should be screened carefully.

Because it's difficult for any one person to adequately understand all the terms, keywords and workflows used by all departments, each department will likely need its own Metadata Editor. (Some departments will have more than one.)

The skills required for this position will depend on the type of metadata that's added to your DAM.

For example, if abstracts, captions or other "essay" metadata values will be seen outside your organization, the Metadata Editor should possess writing skills. If that content is provided by others, the Metadata Editor must at least be able to proofread, verify and edit, if needed.

On the other hand, if all metadata values in your DAM are selected from menus or lists, requiring no writing, the focus of your Metadata Editors should be on the understanding of the content with regard to how it relates to the metadata values available.

The competency of your Metadata Editors will, perhaps more than anything else, affect the usability of your DAM. If the wrong tags are assigned, or if metadata values are misspelled, that's a disaster in terms of DAM. In addition, because metadata can be used to control asset distribution and access, this is a position not ideal for interns.

Doubling Up on Duties

If you're thinking now that DAM will require far too many resources to be useful at your organization, don't panic yet.

While all of the *duties* outlined above are required, it is possible for an individual to cover multiple bases. For example, you might have a Systems Manager who's also capable and willing to serve as your Technical Developer. Or, your Librarian/Archivist might make a great Metadata Editor.

Doubling up on duties is much easier to make work if your DAM initiative is less ambitious. For example, if only one department will be using the DAM, then you might not need a dedicated Database Manager and Metadata Editor. Likewise, if the system won't be accessible to the public, you might—*might!*—be able to get away without having a Metadata Editors at all.

What Happens When Duties Aren't Covered

As mentioned, though you might not have the resources to hire new people to perform these duties, it's imperative that all duties are performed, no matter how small your initiative might be.

If you're not convinced, below is a (over simplified) table that shows what happens over time when one of these duties is ignored.

Missing Duty	Short Term	Long Term
Initiative Owner	No coordination between stakeholders. No progress.	No DAM initiative.
Systems Manager	No access to systems needed for testing, installation and access. No one to work out technical issues with the DAM vendor.	No support when systems go offline or servers fail. Downtime discourages users from wanting to use the DAM.
Librarian or Archivist	No one knows how to start organizing the system, or how to best interview users about their needs.	Finding things is not going to be easy. Users become discouraged and stop using the DAM.
Technical Developer	You're doomed to "out-of-the-box" functionality, which isn't suited to your needs. Your DAM remains an island, because it isn't integrated with other systems.	User requests for system improvements are not addressed. ROI is limited because other systems aren't able to leverage your DAM investment.
Database Manager	Departments have to make do with a generic	Rogue departments decide they're better

	configuration that doesn't address their needs. They can't track the metadata they need, because the appropriate fields are not available.	off running their own DAMs. Your DAM initiative splinters and you eventually lose support entirely.
Metadata Editor	Assets are ingested with little or no useful metadata, or the metadata that's entered remains unchecked and prone to errors.	Users can't find what they need, resulting in frustration. Assets whose licenses have expired aren't taken offline, because no one set the expiration date.

The File Formats You Use

Some DAM vendors like to (constantly) remind prospects that their DAMs support *all* file types. This is supposed to impress you, but it's really an antiquated message that hasn't been interesting in 10 years or more. Today, virtually all professional DAMs can manage any file type.

Far more important than being able to ingest a particular type of file is what users will be able to actually do with those files inside the DAM. More specifically, you want to know what your users will be able to do with the files your organization uses now, or plans to use.

This section lists some popular file types, and offers some suggestions about what you might ask your prospective DAM vendors about their handling of specific formats.

▶ *When I speak of file type, I refer to a general category of file. Within those general categories are specific file formats. For example, "JPEG" is a file format within the file type "images."*

Images (Photographs)

Images are the number one file type for DAM, by far. This is why you'll find the feature sets of most DAM software focused on these files.

Among the most popular file formats of this file type are JPEG, TIF, PNG and PSD, which is the native Adobe Photoshop format. Digital camera "RAW" file formats fall in this category, too.

Below are some things to keep in mind when evaluating a DAM's ability to handle images and photos:

Metadata extraction and write-back – Can the DAM extract all metadata that's embedded inside the file formats you need? If not, what will be missing? Also ask about metadata embedding, or writing metadata back into the images so that it travels with the image after distribution. Not all image formats permit this, but for those that do, the DAM should support it.

Previewing – What preview options are available for your formats? Can you see the original file or just a lower resolution proxy? How quickly do previews appear? Are high-quality previews available over the Web and via mobile interfaces? Can you zoom and pan within the preview with acceptable performance? Can you preview images side-by-side? How easy is that to do?

Processing and repurposing – What processing options are available for each image file format? Can you easily convert between the file formats you need? Can you make content changes, such as color space conversions and watermarking? Are these conversions possible on the fly, or must the converted assets be created ahead of time? Most importantly, how good do the processed images look? Are they of the quality you expect? What options do you have for extending the DAM's image processing functionality? Finally, is there any sort of image editing environment inside the DAM so that users can do interactive tweaking?

Commenting – What's the workflow like for commenting and reviews? Will reviewers need to purchase additional software to see complex images, like Photoshop files? How are comments entered, and how do users know when comments have been entered?

Illustrations and Drawings

These files commonly contain logos or other non-photographic illustrative works, such as signage and line drawings. Adobe Illustrator is the most commonly used application for creating and editing files of this type.

These files are considered "vector art" because they contain mathematical information that describes what software or a printer should render for display or output. These files require special capabilities when it comes to previews and conversions, and not all DAMs do it well, if they can do it at all.

Among the most popular file formats of this type are EPS and AI (Adobe Illustrator). You might also encounter SVG, which is similar in concept to EPS, though far less common.

Below are some things to keep in mind when evaluating DAM software's ability to handle illustrations and drawings:

Metadata and content extraction – Similar to images, which metadata values can be extracted? Can metadata values be written back into the assets too? Some DAMs can also extract the text used in illustrations and make it searchable metadata. This is helpful, because the files can then be found based on text they contain. This is handy, for example, when a print-out is the only information one has about the asset. Without knowing the file's name, or any other associated metadata, users can still find the file based on text they see in the print out.

Previewing – Are previews generated (rendered) on the fly by the DAM, or must the files contain an embedded preview provided by the editing application? If no preview is available, what will users see? If available, are the DAM-rendered previews of a reasonable quality?

Processing and repurposing – Can vector files be converted into high-resolution JPG, TIF or other image formats of any size? Vector art can be scaled to any size without loss of fidelity, so your DAM should be able to convert these files into gorgeous image format files at any size needed. This is also how users would get Web- and presentation-ready versions of your logos and other vector artwork.

Commenting – What's the workflow like for commenting and reviews? Will reviewers need to purchase additional software to see these files, or will the DAM provide everything they need? How are comments entered, and how do users know when comments have been entered?

Word Processing Documents

Among the most popular file formats of this genre are DOC and DOCX, the native file formats of Microsoft Word. Also included in the genre are files created by Apple's Pages application (PAGES), and the OpenOffice (and LibreOffice) Writer application (ODT).

Below are some things to keep in mind when evaluating DAM software's ability to handle word processing documents:

Metadata and content extraction – In addition to all embedded metadata, many DAMs can also extract the entire contents of word processing documents into searchable metadata.

Previewing – Are previews of the word processing files high quality? When previewed, do the documents look the same in the DAM as they do in your word processor? Are previews rendered by the DAM, or is a low-quality preview extracted from the file itself? What will users see if a preview can't be shown? Can users page through a document to see every page it contains?

Processing and repurposing – Can word processing documents be converted to any other formats, such as PDF or another word processor's format? For example, can a Microsoft Word user download an Apple Pages file in Word format? Conversions of these types aren't easy, so consider this a DAM deal-breaker only if you absolutely need this functionality.

Commenting – If you expect to you use your DAM for commenting on word processing documents, make sure per-page comments can be added and easily found. Keep in mind, this isn't something you're likely to find, but things change pretty quickly in the DAM world. You never know what's coming from the more clever vendors.

Presentations

Because "presentation" and "PowerPoint" are often synonymous terms, the most popular presentation formats are PPT and PPTX, the native PowerPoint formats. You might also need to manage files created in OpenOffice Impress (ODP) and Apple Keynote (KEY).

Below are some things to keep in mind when evaluating DAM software's ability to handle presentations:

Ingesting – Some DAMs can create individual database records for each slide in a presentation. This enables users to manage metadata on a per-slide level, and it also (usually) makes it possible to create new presentations that are based on the individual slides of various presentations already inside the DAM.

Metadata and content extraction – As with word processing documents and illustrations, many DAMs can extract the textual contents of presentations, making it easier to find individual slides. In addition, make sure the DAM can capture all the metadata you enter into the presentation itself, such as notes and file info. All captured metadata should be linked to the appropriate slide, and not just dumped into a single database record that represents the entire presentation.

Previewing – Previews should be clear and scalable, and users should be able to page through each slide in a presentation.

Processing and repurposing – Some DAMs can create PDFs and images from presentation slides. This can be helpful, but make sure the PDFs contain the actual text from each slide, and not just a picture rendering of the slides. A rendering might still be useful to you, but it won't enable readers to find content by searching, and the file sizes can be pretty large.

Commenting – Users should be able to add comments on any slide in a presentation, and there should be an easy way for others to find slides that contain comments. If presentations are subject to reviews at your organization, make sure some means for managing reviews is available, and that it works as you'd expect.

Layouts

The most popular file formats of this type are INDD (Adobe InDesign), QXP (QuarkXPress) and FM (Adobe FrameMaker). Others include Adobe PageMaker (PMD and other extensions that have changed over the years) and Microsoft Publisher (PUB).

Below are some things to keep in mind when evaluating DAM software's ability to handle layouts:

Ingesting – Can the DAM create individual database records for each page in the layout? If so, this will make finding individual pages easier, and it will make per-page approvals possible, assuming the DAM also provides some means for conducting reviews and approvals.

Metadata and content extraction – In addition to all the standard metadata considerations, layouts are unique in that they contain or reference other files. Ask if the DAM can reference these other files so that you can track what was used in each layout. Ask also if files not already in the DAM can be automatically ingested when the layout is ingested, or whether the DAM can at least track which files a layout references that are not in the DAM. (So that users can manually ingest those files later.) As with other text documents, the entire text contents of each page should be extracted into searchable metadata. Also ask whether the DAM can extract font and other information that would be helpful for editing the layout on a computer other than the one on which it was created. You'll appreciate this if you need to open a layout that someone else created years ago.

Previewing – Per-page previews should be available, and they should be at least readable. Given the sophisticated nature of layouts, even this might be tough to find. In order to generate an on-the-fly preview, the DAM would have to be able to reference each file the layout contains. Without some integration into external software that can render a layout page, like QuarkXPress Server or InDesign Server, you're not likely to get great previews from your layouts.

Processing and repurposing – With one of the aforementioned server products, a DAM might be able to generate (searchable) PDFs for a layout, or render its individual pages to image files. Without such an integration, you might be able to convert the layout's already low-quality previews into low-quality images, but the purpose for doing so would be limited to creating thumbnails or other small files.

Commenting – Per-page commenting and approvals can be valuable for workflows that involve layouts. Users should be able to add those comments using tools that make it clear to the layout artist where changes are needed.

PDF (Portable Document Format)

PDF files are pretty well supported by most DAMs today, but there are a few tricks some DAMs offer that can be helpful.

Metadata extraction – XMP describes the embedded metadata inside a PDF. Make sure the DAM can extract all of it. By nature, XMP can include many different metadata schemas; so make sure you ask the DAM vendor to what extent XMP is supported. Also ask whether the text contents of the PDF can be extracted into searchable metadata, and whether each PDF page can be represented by its own database record. The DAM should also be able to write metadata back into the PDF file.

Previewing – High-quality PDF previews should be possible because, unlike layouts, PDF files don't (usually) need to reference external files. Make sure the previews look good to you, and that Web and mobile users will be able to see them too. Users should be able to preview each page of a PDF file individually, too.

Processing and repurposing – Due to their already flexible nature, you're not likely going to have a lot of processing needs for your PDF files. You might, for example, want the DAM to create thumbnail images you can use on your website, but this should be easy. Don't expect things like converting PDFs into Word files, layouts or other such formats. This rarely works well, even from within in those applications; it's not reasonable to expect a DAM to be able to do this reliably, if at all.

Commenting – Per-page commenting and approvals should be available. Users should be able to add those comments using tools that make it clear where changes are needed.

Video

You're either using video already, or you will be—I promise. So, whether video is currently high on your priority list, make it a consideration during your DAM evaluations. At the very least, a DAM that doesn't adequately support video well should be considered an antique these days.

The most common video formats include WMV, AVI, MOV, MPEG and FLV. Countless other formats used for video, too; pay close attention to which formats are properly supported by any DAM software you consider.

Ingesting – It's worth specifically asking which video formats can be ingested into a DAM. Also ask from where those videos can come. For example, can you enter a URL from YouTube and have the DAM create a record for that file? This enables your organization to not only index your own videos, but those that come from other sources too—all without the copyright concern of duplicating the files. Ingesting via URL can be valuable for other file formats too, but it's particularly great for video, because you don't want to move these large files if you don't need to.

Metadata extraction – The metadata you'll find inside video files will vary considerably, depending on the file format. At the very least, make sure the DAM can extract frame rate, data rate, total number of frames and the codec used. Of course, consider these values in addition to all the usual metadata you'd expect.

Previewing – Users expect to be able to stream previews of any video they find, regardless of the file's format, codec or data rate. This is a tall order for a DAM, but that's life. At the very least, make sure video previews are clean, smooth and that you can scan around the file at will. (Some codecs and/or formats make scanning difficult or impossible, but the DAM shouldn't be the limiting factor.)

Processing and repurposing – If you need your DAM to be able to convert between video formats, make this the *first* conversation you have with the DAM vendors you contact. Few DAMs do this well, so this could be the single biggest deciding factor as to which software will work for you. Also find out when conversions can take place. Are conversions performed when the video is first ingested? Can users select a video and choose an output format for download? Can they choose a video and have the DAM upload it to YouTube directly? Also find out if new videos can be created from ranges of frames (clips) defined in other videos. If so, see if controls are available to maintain audio levels, match frame sizes or other considerations required to make the output video watchable.

Commenting – If you'll need to conduct DAM-based approvals, make sure comments can be added on a per-frame basis, and that those comments are easy for others to find. Ideally, comments will scroll as the video plays back.

Audio

Before you dismiss audio as a required format, consider all those podcasts out on the Internet. Like video, this is a format whose value is only going to increase over time.

Among the most common audio file formats are MP3, AIF and WAV. You might also come across Real Audio (RA).

Ingesting – As with video, make sure the DAM can ingest the audio formats you'll be using.

Metadata extraction – Also similar to video, audio files contain unique values, such as bit depth, sample rate, length of the recording, number of channels, etc. Make sure all these values are captured in addition to the standard metadata.

Previewing – Users will want to stream audio on demand, rather than having to download the files first. Make sure this is possible, and that it works well. Users should be able to jump to different sections of the audio playback without undo delays or audio stuttering.

Processing and repurposing – Audio conversions are easier than video, but they're still difficult for some DAM systems. An example of when an audio conversion would be needed is when the master audio file has been stored in an uncompressed format, which means the file size might be quite large. If someone needs that content for the purposes of a podcast, it will need to be converted to a smaller file.

Commenting – You'll need some means for commenting on specific sections of an audio file, if this will be part of your workflow. Comments entered about the entire file will likely be of limited use to those who need to make the changes.

3D/CAD Models, Scenes and Animations

A few DAM systems have been optimized for use with 3D and CAD formats. Using these systems, users can spin around 3D models, changing lighting conditions and more. It's lots of fun.

Unfortunately, these systems are sometimes behind the curve when it comes to standard DAM functionality. Because of this, organizations whose workflows are based on 3D or CAD formats often choose to adopt more traditional DAM software.

Among the most common formats in this genre are OBJ, 3DS/MAX, MB/MA (Maya), 3DM (Rhinoceros 3D), DXF and DWG (AutoCAD).

Ingesting – Though most DAMs should be able to accept any 3D file format, it's worth asking DAM vendors about the specific formats you use. For example, .IMG files are used in some 3D production pipelines, but a completely different type of file that uses the same extension is more popular in daily computing. Some DAMs might treat your 3D .IMG files as if they were these other files, which will confuse users. In addition, some 3D formats are actually (very large) text files. When added to your DAM, you want to make sure the system doesn't treat those files as it would a file from a text editor.

Metadata extraction – Without specific support for a given 3D/CAD format, you're not likely to be able to extract much of the metadata the file contains. Unlike the formats commonly used for 2D design, 3D formats are often so different from one another that the various vendors involved don't even bother trying to standardize.

Previewing – The preview of 3D objects requires real-time rendering technologies that virtually no DAM offers natively. I have seen plugins that make this possible, but they are costly additions to already-costly DAMs. How much are you willing to pay so that users can rotate objects?

Workflow and approvals – If the review of 3D files (objects or scenes) is a necessary part of your workflows, chances are those conducting the reviews are already working with software capable of properly displaying the objects, which includes being able to change lighting and surface qualities to test rendering attributes. No serious 3D production would accept anything less as being an "approval" of a 3D work.

Processing and repurposing – If you're hoping to find a DAM that can convert between 3D file formats, you'll be disappointed. 3D format conversion is such a difficult science that entire software packages are dedicated to the process, and even they don't work reliably much of the time.

All these limitations notwithstanding, most modern DAM software will at least be capable of ingesting, adding metadata and archiving your 3D files. But don't plan on using a DAM to enable senior directors confused by basic computing tasks to participate in a 3D approval workflow.

Archives

Though the term "ZIP file" has become synonymous with "archive," other archive formats exist too. An archive file is really no different than any other file; the fact that it contains other files is what's most significant when it comes to DAM. You want your DAM to be able to track all your files, even when those files are inside other files.

Among the most common archive formats in use are ZIP, RAR, TAR and ISO.

Ingesting – Ask vendors how their systems deal with archive files. Some systems will be able to extract and index the files therein. Some DAMs can even index an archive's contained files in place, without having to extract them. Other DAMs will treat archive files no differently than they do any others.

Metadata extraction – In addition to any metadata contained by the archive file itself, find out how the DAM handles the metadata contained inside the files contained in the archive. If the DAM extracts those files and indexes them independently, this shouldn't be any different than if the files were indexed themselves. But if the DAM indexes files inside an archive in place, make sure it can index the metadata those files contain.

Previewing – In theory, there's no meaningful preview to come from an archive, because all the files contain are other files. Still, you might want to be able to preview the files an archive contains. Ask your DAM vendors what's supported on their systems.

Processing and repurposing – The ability to access any file inside an archive is probably the most value processing option you'll have for these files. Some DAMs might also be able to convert between archive formats, but the long-term benefits of such a feature might be limited. For example, if you have a few thousand RAR files that you want to convert to ZIP, you're better off doing that conversion before you add the files to the DAM. Still, conversion between archive formats isn't rocket science, so your favorite DAM system might support it natively, or at least be able to support it via its application programming interface (API).

Web formats

The idea of downloading Web pages and then ingesting them into a DAM might seem absurd, but what about "pointing" your DAM to those pages and having them indexed in place?

You know, like Google does.

With a capability like this, you can extend the approval and communication features of your DAM to your website or blog. It also enables you to have a central content search interface that works across all your Web properties.

Still not convinced? Imagine being able to index the Web pages of a competitor, without that company ever knowing. You could keep an eye on which keywords they're using, which sections they include, what's new, etc. If you really want to get serious, you could add metadata fields for things like Google PageRank or other metrics that suggest the popularity of those pages.

Or, if you're a blogger wondering which topics need coverage, you could use your DAM to search all the pages of competing archives to see which topics are still untouched.

The Web formats you're most likely to be able to add to your DAM are HTML, PHP and XML.

Ingesting – In-place indexing is usually the best option for Web format indexing. As mentioned, you don't want to have to download an entire website just to feed it to your DAM. Also ask your vendor about crawling. In other words, can it follow links and index those pages too? If so, can you prevent the DAM from moving on to other domains, or diving down too many levels? (After all, you're not trying to be Google.)

Metadata extraction – Web pages contain no embedded metadata, as we're used to having in other files. They do, though, contain metadata in tags that appear inside the file with the rest of the content. For example, the HTML meta tag attribute "Description" contains a small chunk of text that's supposed to describe the page. Can your DAM read those meta tags and copy their values into related metadata fields in your DAM? Also, of course, make sure the entire text contents of the page can be extracted into searchable metadata.

Previewing – The DAM should be able to show a preview of a renderable Web page. You'll have to decide whether it would be best to see a real-time preview, or a preview that was cached at the time the page was last indexed.

Processing and repurposing – Creating PDFs of indexed Web pages can be useful. It's a handy way to reference pages in a report, and it gives you a one-click option for creating thumbnails you can use in other sections of your site, or in printed materials.

Commenting – Website development often involves many people, and even more opinions than people. Per-page commenting could be valuable not only during the development phase of your site, but it can offer users a convenient means for reporting trouble they see on live sites. Imagine a link on each of your pages that says, "Click here to report problems with this page." When clicked, your DAM presents the user with a page from which comments can be added, complete with drawn rectangles or other tools to help clarify the comments.

If your website is based on a content management system (CMS), you might find that your CMS already offers some of the functionality described. If so, that's great. But keep in mind, you might benefit from having this functionality for sites other than the ones you own and edit via your CMS.

Font formats

Few people think about fonts until those fonts are needed and the designer who last had them is long gone.

For example, your organization might dutifully index every layout it has produced in the past decade, but unless you have an archive of the fonts used in those layouts, you'll run into trouble if you later have to reassemble the page for reprints or some other use. Even when a font of the same name is available, it might not be identical to the one used in the layout, making odd page- or line-breaks possible.

The three most common font formats in use today are OTF (OpenType Font), TTF (TrueType Font) and PostScript

Ingesting – The most convenient time to index fonts is when indexing a file that uses those fonts. See if your DAM is capable of reading the fonts used in a given document and crosschecking to see if those fonts are already in the DAM. If not, the indexing user should be queried as to whether the fonts should be indexed too. Or, as with layouts, see if there's a way to at least note in the DAM which fonts are used in indexed documents, so they can indexed manually.

Metadata extraction – The metadata you'll need from your fonts includes the copyright info, owner, version number and other values important for being able to positively identify the specific font. If copyright restrictions prevent you from indexing your fonts, you should still be able to index your fonts' metadata. That will offer you a good option for repurchasing or otherwise acquiring those same fonts in the future.

Previewing – Font previews could be valuable if your DAM will be used by designers for font selection. This would enable designers to choose what works best amongst the fonts your organization already owns. If you won't be using the DAM like this, I would consider font previews to be a nice-to-have, but not a need-to-have.

Processing and repurposing – Font conversion isn't that difficult a science, but I haven't seen any DAM software that does this natively. You might, however, be able to add this functionality via a system's API. But, as with archive conversion, this might be something you're better off doing before the files are indexed. This will enable you to take advantage of inexpensive font-conversion utilities available on the Web.

Integrations with Applications

Just as important as the file types you use are the applications you use to create and edit those files.

Some DAM systems offer ways in which users can access the DAM right from within popular applications like Adobe Creative Suite, Microsoft Office and more.

Depending on your workflows, you might find that direct access to your DAM from within production applications can save enormous amounts of time, not to mention how it can help you while you're trying to get buy-in from those who will use the system.

It can also do the exact opposite.

Integration with production applications is a very delicate issue. The most popular applications in use today are popular for a reason—users like the way they work. (Or they're at least used to them.) So, when a DAM vendor sticks DAM-direct functionality inside those applications, it had better solve more problems than it creates.

First off, you have to consider how beneficial direct access is in the first place. How difficult is accessing the DAM ordinarily? If all it takes is an open Web browser, this is a "pain" most creative users are willing to endure. After all, they probably have a Web browser open anyway. On the other hand, if access requires installing 150MB+ native client software for the DAM, that's another issue.

Nothing moves faster than the creative process, even when things appear to not be moving at all. When a designer, author or other creative individual is on a roll, anything that gets in the way is unacceptable—even if that interruption is only momentary. Access to your DAM needs to be invisible to these users. Anything a DAM vendor offers needs to work within the software paradigms and limitations users have already accepted.

If your DAM vendor's QuarkXPress or InDesign integration software is so cumbersome that it forces layout artists to rethink how they find, use and save files, there's no point. No one will want to use it.

Also consider the impact those plugins have on your DAM. For example, if InDesign users just want to browse and access files for use in layouts, will this tie up a user license on your DAM? If you have a five-user InDesign work group and you have a five-user DAM license, you can guess what happens when a sixth person tries to access the DAM.

If an in-application plugin will be part of your DAM workflow, make sure it's tested completely before you make any commitments, to the DAM vendor or your users.

Some application integrations that can be very valuable use the DAM for file control, but use other software for distribution. In other words, the DAM "pushes" approved files to other applications. Alternately, users of other applications "pull" approved files from the DAM using the software interface they know best. I've seen integrations like these for Dropbox, SharePoint, Typo3 (content management system) and a handful of other systems.

These less intrusive types of integrations can be ideal because they offer a clear benefit to the users of those other systems, and they don't require users to relearn anything. Conversely, when a DAM vendor sticks a new palette window or menu option into InDesign, PowerPoint or Word, that vendor is encroaching on what's already a very established set of tools. When done right, users rejoice; otherwise, users rebel.

For a very simple example of how a bad integration can hinder the creative process, consider a typical InDesign workflow:

1. User searches for images inside the DAM.
2. Users places chosen image into the layout.
3. User edits the layout and…then what?

Layout artists are used to saving files to their local machines, or to a local file server. When DAM integrations offer an additional option to add the files to the DAM, what's a user to do? Should the file be saved locally and then added to the DAM? Or, should it be added to the DAM only? Shouldn't the DAM be adding the files automatically?

As simple an example as this is, it underscores how workflow ambiguity can adversely affect productivity. Further considering the example above, what happens if the layout is saved to the DAM but not saved locally? Ideally, the DAM integration should guide the user through what makes the most sense. If the user tries to save the file locally, that integration should provide direction that's easy to understand and remember.

When considering a DAM vendor, don't just accept that the application integrations it promotes will work as you expect. Insist on seeing the software in action. Compare how it actually works to how your users will demand that it work. This is a wonderful example of why you should make no software decisions without a representative of your users involved.

Asset Processing

Most DAM software offers at least some digital asset processing options, but no DAM does everything. As part of your initiative planning, determine exactly what type of asset processing you'll need. Add these requirements to your global requirements, and carefully test each DAM you evaluate to make sure it does what you need.

Also make sure the files a DAM produces are useable in your applications, and that they contain all the metadata you expect. Files that look okay on the surface can sometimes contain errors you wouldn't know about unless you tried to actually work with those files in your editing application.

During your DAM evaluations, make sure you see all of the following first hand:

- Do the resulting (processed) files look/sound good?
- How are the processing options configured?
- Can you reserve certain processing options for certain users or groups?
- Which processing library is in use?

I cannot stress that first point enough. Some DAM vendors make wild claims about the processing options their software offers. While those systems might (technically) offer what's promised, the resulting quality of those processed files can be downright unusable.

For example, one DAM I've used is advertised to be able to convert RGB images to CMYK. (RGB is the color space used for computer screens; CMYK is used for print.) Technically, this DAM *can* do RGB-to-CMYK color space conversions, but the resulting files are useless.

When converting to CMYK, you need to know the target output device. This enables you to choose the correct color profile so that the converted files appear in print close to how they appear on screen. (Users of Photoshop will know what I mean.) This particular DAM offered no means for choosing a color profile for the conversion, which made the resulting files suitable only for some theoretical generic output device that didn't exist.

"Can you do this" isn't the only question you should ask a DAM vendor when it comes to asset processing. Demand to see proof, right before your own eyes.

Once you are certain a given DAM can do the processing you need, and you're happy with the quality of the resulting files, you next need to find out how those processing jobs are configured.

In most DAMs, system administrators can preconfigure processing options that are presented to users as menu options or buttons. For example, one menu that read, "Download for Presentations." This processing configuration would presumably down-sample larger images, the save them into a file format suitable for presentations.

Preconfigured options save users from having to know anything about the conversion process, which makes them a wonderful addition to the DAM.

The trick, of course, lies in the configuration itself. In some systems, configurations are created using UI (user interface) elements that are pretty easy to understand. Other systems rely on text-file based configurations that can be challenging. Other systems require a little of both.

If configuring a processing option in a DAM you evaluate proves to be something that only your Technical Developer will be able to do, make sure you have a Technical Developer. (Or choose another DAM.)

Also consider which on-the-fly processing functionality you want to make available to users, if any. The benefit here is that users can make choices that better reflect a specific use for the downloaded file.

The downside is that untrained users can get themselves into trouble. For example, someone might try to upscale a small JPEG into a 50 megabyte monster because she figures it will look bigger when projected onto a big screen from her presentation. You know, make it HD and all that.

Further, some processing options will require information your average user won't know.

For example, when converting a video for use on the Web, considerations like maximum data rate and codec are extremely important. But most users will have no idea which options to choose. Instead, most DAM users would prefer to just tell the DAM where they intend to use the video clip, and let the DAM figure it all out.

This is a classic case of balancing flexibility with ease of use. It's great to be able to let users choose how large a downloaded image should be, but it's even better to build in some logic that warns the user when the parameters entered make no sense.

If you do want to let trained users make some choices, at least make sure the more obscure settings are hardwired into the processing configuration. Go ahead and let users choose a basic size, but when it comes to determining data rates and codecs for video, for example, it's probably better for the DAM to determine those values based on the user's intended use.

For example, don't offer a menu that offers the following options:

- Maximum Data Rate: 100kps; H.264
- Maximum Data Rate: 400kps; FLV

Instead, offer something like this:

- Download for Mobile Streaming
- Download for YouTube

You're still giving users some control, but you're hiding the confusing things.

Some DAMs also offer embedded image editing environments that enable users to crop into areas of a photo, or make manual adjustments to color, hue, etc.

I've seen these built-in editors range from being barely usable to being quite impressive. On smarter systems, presets enable users to focus on content rather than metrics. For example, a menu option called "Crop for Website Banner" would present a properly sized crop box that the user could place wherever needed.

Next, find out how to determine which user or group can access each processing option.

In some cases, your goal will be to make things easier for users by not offering them choices they'll never use. For example, the processing options salespeople need will likely be far more basic than those required by designers. Even when the processing is exactly the same, you might want to still use different names for the option, depending on the target group: "Download for Web" for salespeople; "JPEG, 600px max" for designers.

In other cases, you'll want to restrict access to processing options for security reasons.

Say you sell images from your DAM. You want users to be able to browse your collection to find what they need, but you won't want them to be able to download original files until payment has been processed.

This problem is solved by making your sample or "for position only" (FPO) files available only through a processing option that down-samples and then watermarks downloaded files. Anyone who's downloading files as a guest, or a customer who has not licensed a selected file, will receive a processed version. This is a standard practice at commercial photo houses.

Your watermark could even include contact and purchase information, which will help ensure layout artists and others always know where to go to buy the image. Once payment is processed, you can provide a download link that performs no processing.

Another type of restriction has more to do with common sense than it does security. If a user has selected an audio file for download, you don't want that user to be able to choose among processing options suitable only for images. This will confuse users, or result in an error instead of a download. Either outcome will reflect poorly on the professionalism and usability of your DAM.

Users should be able to choose an appropriate processing option for each downloaded file, even when files are downloaded in batches that contain several file formats.

Global processing options, such as packing all selected files into a Zip or other archive format, should also be available.

Lastly, find out which digital processing library the vendor is using. Some vendors use industry standard libraries that are well supported and regularly improved, while others use a proprietary library they control.

In my experience, industry standard libraries, like GraphicsMagick and ImageMagick, provide better quality and flexibility that the libraries DAM vendors provide. After all, how many things can one DAM vendor do well? If DAM is the vendor's main focus, chances are its processing library will be lacking. (More on the value of standards later.)

The other advantage to using standard libraries is that you'll be able to find people other than your DAM vendor to improve them for you. Whereas a vendor might want thousands of dollars to add a requested function, you might find developers on the Web who are willing to do it for a fraction of that cost, and in far less time. Better still, what you need might have already been developed, and it might be free for the asking.

Digital processing is one of the best reasons to adopt a DAM system. Just make sure you carefully determine your asset processing needs, and then compare those needs to what can each DAM you evaluate can deliver.

Asset Publishing and Distribution

When it comes to DAM, people like to think in terms of publishing assets or distributing them. Because these terms are so often used interchangeably, I prefer to think in terms of "Pull" and "Push" as our primary distribution methods.

Pull distribution (publishing) describes files sitting patiently waiting for people to request them. A download link on a website is an example of Pull distribution. Requesting a file directly from a DAM is another example.

Push distribution describes sending a copy of an asset to a recipient or location, either as an email attachment, a file on a DVD, or some other method of delivery.

Pull distribution is most suitable for assets that are published in support of other content. For example, a software company's product page might offer a PDF download that details the technical requirements of the software. The product information content on the page is the main draw, while the downloadable asset plays only a supporting role.

Push distribution offers a more direct, aggressive way of getting assets into the hands of those you want to have them. For example, when a new product is released, some companies email a product information sheet to customers and prospects. Organizations might also burn DVDs that are mailed.

As obvious an option as Push distribution might seem, its value has diminished. First off, pushing assets out, no matter which way you do it, requires effort and potentially significant costs.

Further, once a file has been sent, it's gone—there's no "unsend" option. If you find you've sent the wrong version, or the file contains some errors, the best you can do is redistribute the file with an apology.

When it's time to update a previously "pushed" file, your only option is to resend it. This can result in multiple versions stored on users' local computers, which can lead to confusion.

And when you do send files via email, email servers might reject them. SPAM and virus filters are more likely to flag files that contain attachments, and some email servers will reject files that are above a certain size limit.

As disaster prone as I've made Push distribution seem, it's still far preferable to passively putting a valuable digital asset on your website and hoping someone shows up to download it.

Fortunately, there's a hybrid approach so simple in concept that you might have already thought about it: Push an *announcement* about the asset via email or social media, and include a link to download the asset directly from your DAM.

One of the greatest benefits of this approach is that you retain control over the files recipients download. Sure, once people download the file, they have a copy. But at least you can fix typos and update the file, knowing that all future downloads from that same link will lead to the most recent version of the file.

This hybrid type of distribution offers the best of Push and Pull distribution.

Consider a price list you provide on your website. At some point, the document will need an update. Using Pull distribution alone, you'd update the file and then have to just hope people came back to download fresh copies. Push distribution would send out new copies, but then you'd have to worry about file attachments getting lost, or recipients being confused by having multiple versions of the file.

Using the hybrid approach, you simply update the master copy in your DAM and leave it at that. All links to the file that will now retrieve the updated version. If you need to alert previous downloaders, your DAM might be able to help, if it tracks download statistics, or offers a subscription option that automatically notifies people when files are updated.

The benefits of this are significant when you deal with partners. For example, say you have hundreds of partners or affiliates who use your price list. If you previously sent the price list via Push, those partners would have taken that file, shared it around the office, and perhaps even posted it on their websites. When you next update the file, you're looking at a logistical nightmare to get all those partners to refresh all those copies.

Instead, if you use the hybrid approach, partners can always access the list from the link you send. They can even post this same link on their websites. You can update the file when you need, and everyone will have fresh content the very next time they access that link.

For even greater benefit to you, Google and other search engines rank websites, in part, based on the number of "back links" that point to them. So while you're doing your partners a service by not making them update file copies, you're doing your own website a favor by increasing its number of inbound links.

It's worth noting that in order to derive all these benefits, policy is required. For example, what's to stop all your partners from downloading the file behind your link and copying it to their websites? In truth, they could. But if you have policy in place that forbids the practice, this can become part of your agreement with partners. It's an example of where DAM policy flows into many other aspects of business.

If this hybrid approach sounds like something that will make sense for your organization, make sure the DAM software you choose is capable of generating and managing DAM-direct download links to your assets. Equally important, make sure the DAM you choose is effectively integrated into social media.

Lastly, as always, ask to see exactly how this workflow would work. What configurations are required? How is the file behind the link updated? How are asset subscriptions handled? How easy is it to accomplish?

Some DAMs might offer the functionality you need, but present it to users in such an awkward way that they'd never use it.

Social Media Meets DAM

Social media integration is important because nothing in the world is gaining popularity faster. If you think social media isn't appropriate for your industry or organization, I'm asking you to think again. As "these kids today" grow into management and decision-making positions, social media will increasingly replace today's traditional methods of distributing information and files.

To put into perspective how this transition is already underway, let me ask you a few questions:

- Do you know how much it costs to place a business ad in your local phone book?
- Do you know your local newspaper's demographics or ad lead times for advertising?
- When was the last time you considered buying television or radio ad time?
- When was the last time your organization sent a direct mail piece through postal mail?

It wasn't that long ago that these options dominated the advertising and information distribution trade. Today, you're probably more focused on email announcements and distribution. And though email is great, let me predict here and now that email is merely a transition technology between phone book ads and social media.

Simply put, you want to make your announcements and files available in the places those you want to reach go to get and share information. This is the nature of advertising. Today, the "right" places are increasingly Facebook, Google+, LinkedIn and similar social sites. There is no more convenient or cost effective means of making people aware of your digital assets than social media. Again, email is great, but it won't be long until social media becomes your default means for making announcements, if it isn't already.

What this means for you today is that your DAM initiative and DAM software must be social media-savvy. If you evaluate DAM software that's not yet fully integrated into social media, look elsewhere. DAM vendors have had plenty of time to figure out the future. Those that are not yet socially integrated are simply not paying attention.

When we think of a DAM initiative, we think in terms of something your organization will be using for many years, if not indefinitely. That in mind, do you think the value of Yellow Pages advertising will increase any time soon? Unless your primary focus is hyperlocal advertising, think bigger about the reach of your DAM and consider social media in all your DAM-related decisions.

Some DAM vendors claim their software can be used for digital asset distribution via social media, but this claim is meaningless without specifics.

For example, if the DAM can generate a download link that you can post into a social feed, that's great, but it's only one part of the equation. Your DAM needs to be able to *really* integrate with those social accounts, meaning it can control the announcement of the release as well as the release itself.

For example, when a media release embargo expires, you want your DAM to release the file. But unless someone knows about that file, it's not going to see much action in terms of downloads. A fully socially integrated DAM should be able to generate a link to that file and create a new post on your social feeds all at the same time. Anything short of this is not full social media integration.

You could certainly make all those posts yourself, but why not let the DAM take care of *all* aspects of distributing your digital assets? By the time that release goes out, you've moved on to other things. You don't want to have to mark your calendar to remember to feed Facebook, Google+ and all the rest.

The future of "Social DAM" will move social media further upstream into the DAM production workflow. Notifications like, "it's your turn to work on the file," will be posted to social accounts rather than just sent via email. And while this will be quite a departure from where things are now, it's only the beginning.

Where we'll really see DAM's social shift is in workflow methodology. Today, most organizations see workflow as a series of linear steps through which asset development occurs. For example, once a draft is created, it's sent for review; if revisions are needed, it's sent back to editorial. The process occurs, one step at a time, until development is complete and the asset is released.

Some organizations, however, prefer a nonlinear, more collaborative approach to production. In these workflows, files are created, edited, routed and approved based on discussion, opinion and popularity more than predefined directive.

For example, when an initial draft of an illustration has been created, it becomes *ready for discussion*, not *ready for approval*. A entire team considers the work, not just a single approver. A designer on that team might have an idea that she adds, creating a new version of the asset for further discussion. Others might do the same. At some point, be it via group discussion or vote, a directive for further development comes.

While this sort of development might seem chaotic to some, for others, collaboration offers a more creative approach to digital asset development.

This shouldn't be an alien a concept, though even if you consider yourself Old School. When you "Like" or "+1" something, you participate in a collaborative process. Your vote influences others, just as previous votes might have influenced you to notice the story, image or whatever it was.

All that in mind, set aside your Old School ways for a moment and consider how an organization might benefit from social collaboration:

An initial logo idea for "Jerry's Kosher Juices" has been created and posted for discussion. Designers rave about its gorgeous lines, while marketing folks praise its punchy appearance. Even client Jerry is beside himself with excitement. Then the front office receptionist, who speaks, reads and writes fluent Mandarin, adds a comment to the discussion thread in which she says the logo looks dangerously close to the Chinese character for "fail."

The point to social interaction is that everyone has an opinion, and many people are experts in at least something.

Why not leverage every resource you have?

If workflow collaboration sounds like something that will work at your organization, your DAM options are limited right now. Few DAM vendors offer any reasonable *linear* workflow tools, let alone functional collaborative options.

But if you add this to your DAM wish list, you'll at least be better able to judge which vendors are most likely to get there first, based on where they are now.

DAM and CMS

As mentioned, term *content management system* (CMS) describes software that provides an edit-friendly, nontechnical interface to a website or blog. CMS software enables those without Web development experience to add and modify published content using a word processor-like interface. CMS also makes it easier for teams to manage content updates collectively. Blogger and WordPress are examples of popular and simple CMS software. More complex CMS power is available from Typo3, Drupal and Joomla.

Where CMS doesn't help (as much) is when images and other non-text assets are needed. Typically, those files must be uploaded into the CMS for inclusion on the Web page.

If an image you want to use on the Web is inside your DAM, you'll have to download the file to your computer and then upload it again into your CMS. If the master image inside the DAM is ever updated, you'll have to go through the entire process again. Will you remember all the places in which that image was used?

Users of CMS and DAM rightfully ask why they can't just pull the images they need directly from the DAM. After all, they've spent all that time adding files to the DAM, adding and editing metadata, and securing approvals. Now, after all that work, they must download the files to their computers only to have to upload them again into the CMS?

To bridge these two worlds, integrations between DAM and CMS systems have been developed. Users create their CMS content as usual, but when an image or other asset is needed, they can find and pull it right from their DAM.

With some integrations, links to asset previews and downloads are embedded into the Web page, mimicking the hybrid distribution model. In other words, when someone opens the Web page or clicks a download link, the DAM serves up fresh copies of all assets used on the page.

Other integrations copy files from the DAM into the server directories where the CMS finds them. This file-copy approach is definitely less sexy, but some CMS software requires the images it uses to be stored in a certain location.

CMS and DAM make for an obvious partnership that really begs an obvious question: *Why can't one system do it all?*

If you ask a CMS vendor, they'll tell you they *can* do it all. Likewise, some DAM vendors claim that all you need is what they offer.

The truth is, while both sides are adding features that encroach on the other's territory, no system has crossed the line entirely, or even adequately. What we have is crude DAM functionality tacked onto CMS, and crude CMS hacked into DAM.

If you're already using a CMS, look for a DAM that offers an integration to that system. If you can't find one, at least look for a DAM that offers an integration with *some* CMS. Given how similar CMS systems are technologically, it shouldn't be difficult for a vendor who adequately supports one CMS to build an interface to another.

Website Integration

In addition to the integration options available for CMS, DAM integrations for non-CMS websites are available too.

At the most basic level, some DAM software can generate standard HTML links that can display image thumbnails or offer downloads. These links are used in Web page code so when the page loads, the image is displayed. Or, as with the hybrid distribution model, when a download link is clicked, the file is served from the DAM.

There are some important benefits to having your DAM provide the images and downloads for your website. First off, you gain some control over the content that appears on the Web. For example, you can configure your DAM so that images not approved for Web use don't even appear as options for your website editors.

Further, if a previously published image must be taken offline, you can do so by making a simple metadata change in the DAM, without having to track down where the image might have been copied to on your Web servers.

If you plan to use your DAM for website integration, make sure it's easy for your website editors to get the links they need, and make sure you'll be able to redirect existing links to other digital assets, so that taking an image offline won't result in dead links.

A more sophisticated approach to integrating your website with your DAM involves embedding an interactive portal to your DAM right inside your website. In other words, users open a website page and they see a simplified DAM interface (portal) appear as an element on that page. The portal provides search fields and other such tools, and assets are displayed within the boundaries of the portal.

The DAM portal is a nice approach, because it provides an interactive DAM experience that enables Web visitors to find and access anything they need. If you need to publish a few thousand files, imagine the benefit of using a DAM portal over having to add and manage a few thousand website hyperlinks.

Physical Media (DVD, CD, tape)

When it comes to distributing digital assets, the need for physical media has lessened. But this doesn't mean there isn't still a place for physical media distribution in DAM.

The Internet offers a convenient and cheap means for moving data, but it's not always the best choice.

Consider the following:

- Large files can take a long time to transfer.
- Long file transfers are prone to errors that might require restarting the transfer.
- Files can appear to have been transferred properly, but without using checksum software to compare the original and transferred copies, file corruption might go unnoticed until the file is needed. (More on that later.)
- Large numbers of files might need to be archived into a single large file, or split into a multi-part archive before they can be transferred successfully.

If you'll be working with larger files that you'll need to transfer to clients, ask DAM vendors how their systems work with physical media. In addition to just copying files onto the physical media, your DAM should be able to update the database record to reflect the move. That way, those who look for the files in the future will know where they went, and when.

If you see physical media distribution in your future, make sure your DAM can integrate with the physical media devices you need. For example, if you plan to copy files to DVDs, make sure your DAM can load the files into a staging area and burn the DVD. If you'll be using tape, make sure your DAM can control the tape machine by loading new tapes and, of course, writing files to tape.

In all cases, your DAM should be able to verify the integrity of all copied files. (More on that later.)

Software Considerations

Though a number of software considerations have already been covered, this section will focus on software specifics that span many diverse purposes, or are so important that they bear calling out into their own discussions.

Cloud or Computer Room

Software you install on one of your own computers is considered "on-premise," meaning it's running on the premises of your organization. Popular applications like Microsoft Office and the Adobe Creative Suite are on-premise software solutions (for now).

Software that runs "in the Cloud" is installed on computers someone else owns and manages. Facebook and Gmail are popular Cloud-based examples.

Some organizations opt for a hybrid of the two: They purchase an on-premise software license and have someone else manage the software for them. This is called *hosted* software.

Cloud and on-premise DAM software is available, which is good, because each has its advantages and weaknesses, and most organizations don't really have a choice when it comes to deciding between these software types. Circumstances or regulations often dictate which option is best, or even acceptable.

It's important to fully understand the pros and cons of each type, and to be able to reconcile those with your own requirements.

On-premise software, being the traditional software model we know best, offers the following advantages:

Control – When software is in your hands, you determine when updates will be installed, and you decide on which computers you'll run the software. You might also have more control over the software's technical configuration, which can be important for some organizations.

Performance – Because the software and your assets are presumably coming from a computer on your organization's local area network (LAN), better file transfer performance can be expected. This can be particularly important if you're working with larger files that might take some time to download over the Internet.

Security – With on-premise software, only those you permit to connect to your network and server can access the software and your data. This is important for organizations that feel they can protect their data better than a third party company.

Long-term costs – Though on-premise software is typically more expensive at first, it can end up costing less over time if no monthly fees are required. If you want the advantage of ongoing software updates, however, you'll likely be locked into monthly or annually recurring fees that can be costly.

On-premise software disadvantages include:

Maintenance – Software that runs on your computers is your responsibility. When things go wrong (and they will), you're at the mercy of your IT team and the technical support department of your software vendor. Your support request goes into a queue where it's handled in some order that's probably not in your favor. This will cost you time while you deal with getting things fixed, and it could cost you significant money in terms of lost revenue and production downtime.

Upgrades – On-premise software purchases rarely include software fixes and updates after the first year. So if you want to avoid using today's software version in 5 years, you need to pay for a software maintenance contract, which can be extremely expensive. One well known DAM vendor charges almost 30% of the total cost of its system for annual maintenance! This means that in just over three years, those customers have paid for their systems twice. What's worse, as you add extra modules and features to the system, your annual maintenance costs increase—forever—even if you later stop using that extra functionality.

Slower evolution – On-premise software developers package updates and bug fixes into release cycles that can span 6 months to 2 years, which can put users at a disadvantage. For example, you might be willing to wait a year for a new feature, but what about a bug fix? Some customers in distress have had to wait many months or more for desperately needed software fixes, simply because their on-premise vendor would not issue interim big-fix patches without being paid for them. Imagine how happy customers are at the idea of paying a vendor to fix its own mistakes.

Global access limitations – When your on-premise software is installed on a machine in Sydney, and your customer is in New York, the reach of that on-premise system becomes a burden. Web interfaces are available for on-premise DAMs, but distance affects performance over the Internet.

Cloud software comes with its own strengths and weaknesses. First, the advantages:

Easy startup – With no software to install, and no complicated configurations to wrestle, Cloud DAMs can be up and running in a matter of minutes.

IT independence – IT departments don't usually get involved with the Cloud software their departments use. They provide Internet access and best wishes—the rest is up to you. This can be an advantage if your IT department doesn't have time to respond to your needs, or if you don't have an IT department. In some cases, I've seen IT departments recommend Cloud-based systems because they didn't want to deal with the installation and maintenance of an on-premise alternative.

Affordable startup costs – Because you're not purchasing the software you'll be able to get into the software for less. (Think rent vs. own.) This can be important when your budget is limited, or your management is in a wait-and-see mode with regard to offering more funding for DAM.

Modern architectures – Cloud software is typically built on more modern architectures than on-premise systems. I say "typically" only because on-premise software that's based on modern software architectures wouldn't be that difficult to migrate to a Cloud-based solution. So any DAM system that's still not available in a Cloud version is likely mired in yesteryear technologies.

Fast updates – When a Cloud vendor fixes a bug, there's no reason to wait extended periods of time before rolling it out to customers. This is particularly true of priority bugs that affect system stability. Cloud vendors can move faster on fixes and updates because they need to make their software run properly on only one computer—their own.

Progressive, innovative thinking – Cloud vendors, in my experience, are often staffed with more forward thinking designers and engineers. "Cloud" is hip and modern, so it attracts the brightest minds in software development.

No software to install – Virtually every computer and mobile device today has a Web browser on board. So with Cloud systems, your DAM login and password are all you need to get your work done. Think about the convenience this affords customers, partners and others outside your organization, not to mention you.

Cloud computing has its disadvantages too:

Performance – Downloading large files over the Internet can really slow things down in your workflow. If your organization already has a slow Internet connection, you can expect users who need to regularly access 500MB Photoshop files to voice their frustrations.

"Cloud escape" plans – There's no option to stop paying for Cloud systems. Once you stop paying, your vendor turns off your access. This is an important consideration if you're worried about the viability of your DAM budget. If this *is* a concern, make sure you choose a DAM vendor that also offers an on-premise version of their Cloud software. This might come in handy if you ever need to escape from the Cloud, or even if you just one day find that on-premise deployment will work better for you.

Long-term costs – Cloud systems charge customers for storage space and network bandwidth. So the more files you have, and the more use your DAM sees, the more expensive the system becomes. These concerns are very real, at least for now. However, I think it's reasonable to expect the costs of storage and bandwidth to continue to decline. Plus, if I'm right that in the future we'll be working with content and not files, users won't be downloading anything—everything will stay in the Cloud, from the moment it's created to the many times it's consumed. Nevertheless, for now you need to consider "cost of ownership" carefully.

Scheduled downtime – Cloud vendors are usually pretty good about advising users when system maintenance is scheduled, but those advisories don't help much if the DAM will be taken offline the day before your big deadline. Fortunately, most Cloud maintenance periods last only an hour or so.

Security – System security is the thing on-premise vendors like to focus on when they need to do some Cloud bashing. They warn that when your metadata and assets are in the Cloud, they're available to virtually any hacker at any time. Granted, this is a scary proposition, but it doesn't make me cancel my online banking and investment accounts. It also doesn't dissuade me from emailing friends and family via Gmail. Online banking, Gmail, Yahoo! Mail, Salesforce, Facebook and LinkedIn are all Cloud-based too. But because security is a significant concern for Cloud systems like these and others, the world's best computer scientists are working on making it better every day.

Regulations – Some companies and countries have regulations in place that govern where and how data can be stored. In some cases, you might not even have the option to use a Cloud system. For example, organizational policy might require that all data be stored on site using computers managed by your IT department. Additionally, some governments mandate that the data of their companies must be stored within the country's political boundaries. Check with your IT managers to find out whether any such restrictions will affect you. This is another reason to consider a vendor that offers Cloud and on-premise options: You never know when the rules will change.

At this point, you probably understand better why the "choice" between on-premise DAM and Cloud DAM isn't usually a real choice. But if any ambiguity still exists, below are some of the more common reasons I have heard for the choice of one versus the other.

Concern	Solution	Rationale
We don't have an IT team or anyone on hand to manage software for us.	Cloud	On-premise software will never be maintenance free. If you don't have someone on hand to manage the software for you, Cloud is your best

		option.
We have a relatively slow Internet connection and we primarily work with Photoshop files and video.	On-premise	If you'll be transferring large files to and from your DAM, on-premise is usually a better option. No matter how fast Internet access is, LAN speeds will virtually always be faster. That said, if you'll be working with video in your DAM without having to download it locally, such as when you're approving clips for YouTube, a Cloud DAM could be ideal.
We don't have a lot of startup money to spend.	Cloud	You'll undoubtedly get into a Cloud system for less money, but carefully consider those longer term costs.
We need total, lock-down control over our metadata and assets.	On-premise	If your organization says there's no room for even the most remote chance of a security breach, then on-premise is a better option. If you are told this, however, do some investigation to make sure your organization uses no other Cloud software that also violates this policy. As mentioned, online banking is Cloud-based, and so are many CRM and accounting systems.
We need convenient, anywhere access to our system for customers, partners and remote employees.	Cloud (Or on-premise with a fully featured Web UI.)	I give the nod here to Cloud only because a system that relies on its Web interface is more likely to have a better, more usable Web interface. If a Web interface is just an alternate to a primary interface, which is common with some on-premise DAMs, it's not likely to offer all the features you'll need, or work the way

		you expect.
We need to integrate with other Cloud systems, such as Salesforce, a content delivery network (CDN) or even a Cloud-based processing engine.	Cloud	The entire point to Cloud computing is that multiple systems can work together to provide a greater benefit. For this reason, Cloud-to-Cloud integration is a perfect reason to adopt a Cloud DAM.
We need to integrate with other on-premise systems, such as DVD burners or inventory control systems.	Cloud or on-premise	Though you might think the win here would go to on-premise, some Cloud systems are capable of integrating with on-premise software just as easily as they can other Cloud systems.
We have a budget to spend on DAM this year, but that might be gone next year.	On-premise	If DAM needs to be a one-time purchase, on-premise is your only option. Keep in mind, this means no software updates, and probably no technical support. But, still, if the well runs dry, you'll at least have the first version of the software you purchased—bugs and all.
We can't wait many months for bug fixes, because our productions are time critical.	Cloud	No DAM software will be bug free. But if you need fixes and updates as soon as possible, Cloud software is a better bet. This will of course vary depending on the vendor. (Ask those user communities!) Cloud vendors can sometimes squash bugs faster because their software is running on a single system configuration that they know well. On-premise vendors often take the "it works for us"

		defense against reported bugs they cannot reproduce. Nothing is more aggravating. On the other hand, if you're willing to pay, you might be able to convince an on-premise vendor to build a bug-fix patch for you.
We want total control over the way our DAM appears and behaves.	On-premise	Total custom system configuration is a double-edged sword. Making your DAM look and behave exactly as you need is great. But it's also going cost a lot of money, and it will make your DAM "nonstandard." This can become an issue when it comes to bug tracking and updates. Vendors are more apt to disregard or delay fixing bugs associated with nonstandard systems. Plus, when a new version of the software comes out, it might not work with all your customizations. Still, there's a better chance you'll be able to completely tweak an on-premise system, because it's yours to do with as you choose. This, of course, is dependent on whether the software provides any configuration options at all—many don't. Cloud systems usually offer limited configuration options, if they offer any at all. But you really need to determine the importance of system tweaks. In my experience, very few DAM customers really make any significant changes to their systems.

License Models

In addition to the Cloud and on-premise software types, you'll hear the DAM industry talking about *open source*, *SaaS*, and *perpetual* software license models too. The type of license you have will define the way in which you'll pay for your DAM software.

Here's a high-level overview of each:

Open source – The software is available at no charge, though "free" rarely ends up being the result.

SaaS – You pay a relatively small setup fee after which you pay per month or year for as long as you use the software.

Perpetual – You pay up front for the entire costs of the software, though ongoing maintenance contracts are extra.

Open source software development is supported by a community effort. This means that updates and bug fixes come from volunteers across the globe who invest time and skills to develop and support the software.

I love the concept behind this software model, but open source software is not always an exercise in the good of humanity. Different factions can evolve within the greater community, and a "we can do this better" sentiment can splinter development into two or more versions of virtually same software.

While this can result in a wonderful boost of innovation and progress, it can also pose a challenge for organizations that have wrapped the software around core business processes. Things can get awkward, like they are when you try to stay in touch with a couple after a bitter divorce.

ImageMagick versus GraphicsMagick offers a great example of this problem. Where there was once a single organization at the fore of open source digital asset processing, now there are two. Though we'd all wish both of these organizations the best, it's likely that only one will prevail in the long run.

Will the winner be the one with which you've aligned yourself?

Though this is certainly less of a concern for a graphics library, imagine the magnitude of code splintering if it was to happen to your entire DAM system.

You also have to concern yourself with continued community interest. While an open source project is the flavor of the month, development can move along nicely. But once the project has aged, the interest of its community of developers can wane. This is particularly true if a competing open source project has come into favor.

Again, this is great for the general advancement of technology, but it can leave those who have adopted the software alone to fend for themselves.

As mandated by open source licenses (and suggested by its name), the source code for open source software is available for anyone to see. (Source code is the text that programmers write that tells the computer how the program functions. It's like a recipe for the software.)

Readily available source code is what makes community development possible, but it can also be a disadvantage too.

If you were a hacker who wanted to figure out how to break into a given open source program, it would be helpful to see the program's source code. Using that code, you could search for code errors you could exploit. (And all software has them.) Using the source code like a road map of weaknesses, you could plan your attack.

Of course, open access to source code also enables well intentioned developers to search for those same exploits so they can be fixed before anyone does any harm.

The Linux kernel is the premiere example of open source development. And though the source code for that kernel is available to anyone, untold millions of installations of operating systems based on Linux are in use worldwide. In fact, your online banking is probably based on Linux.

Nonetheless, the notion of protecting information using code that's available to anyone is just too horrifying for some organizations to consider. For some, corporate policy prevents the use of open source applications. Call it an obsolete view on modern technology, if you will. But you might also consider it a reasonable preventative measure based on the fact that not all open source software is as well developed and tested as the Linux kernel.

The most common misconception about open source that I've seen is that open source means free. Though the software itself might be available at no charge, that doesn't mean you'll be able to do anything with that software without some technical assistance.

More than any other type of software, the use of open source software will require that you have experts on hand to deal with installation, configuration and maintenance. This is because few open source DAMs come packaged as user friendly applications that are ready to go right after download.

In fact, DAM vendors that offer open source software know this very well. After all, if the software a vendor offers is free, how can that vendor stay in business? Paid-for services can be considered as necessary for the successful deployment of open source DAM as electricity is for the machines on which that software will run.

SaaS (software as a service) describes what we usually equate with Cloud software: Someone else runs a system on which we get an account the moment we swipe our credit card. We also expect low startup costs, a low monthly service fee and, of course, no software maintenance hassles.

But these are not the most important advantages SaaS can offer. SaaS software should also be able to take real-time advantage of available processing resources to ensure better performance for users.

This means when the workload increases, SaaS software "borrows" processing power from the server farm on which it runs. When demand drops, the software frees up those extra processors for other software threads to leverage.

The benefit of this is that user requests can be prioritized more intelligently. For example, a user editing metadata fields doesn't really require real-time performance. When a record is saved, it's perfectly fine for that action to take a second or two. But a user previewing video wants playback to occur without hiccups or stalls. Likewise, if your DAM is feeding images to your website, you don't want page load times to skyrocket just because your DAM is busy working on something else.

Properly designed SaaS software knows how to instruct microchips to gang up to power through processor-intensive threads. When the work is done, the chips move on to other tasks, or return to an idle state, awaiting their next assignment.

Contrast this to running software on one of your own machines. Even if your server has four or more processors, that's *all* it has—no matter what the workload. Invite a few hundred thousand users to hammer on your DAM over the Web, and your killer server might become so overloaded, you could add a rotisserie attachment to it and cook a pig.

SaaS software should also be to take advantage of Cloud-level interfaces to other software in order to enhance its own capabilities.

For example, when a user requests a YouTube-ready version of an HD broadcast video, a SaaS DAM should be able to offload the request to other Cloud software that's designed to do such a conversion, without the user having any idea that another system has been called to duty.

Software interoperability like this will become increasingly common, which is why I'm not so concerned about the performance issue of downloading files from the Cloud to the desktop. It won't be long before we see Cloud-based versions of Photoshop and other processing intensive applications. You'll open a Web browser that will provide an interface to everything that's happening in the Cloud. You'll create new files, conduct reviews, and share and distribute that content, all without ever downloading a thing.

If you doubt me, you haven't yet played with Adobe Photoshop Express.

As mentioned, *hosted software* usually describes perpetually licensed software that's managed by another company. The benefit to customers is that they don't need to maintain the systems themselves. The downsides of this model, however, can be significant.

First of all, if you hire someone to host your perpetually licensed software, you'll still have to pay for that expensive upfront perpetual license. But you'll also be paying a monthly fee to the hosting company, and this is in addition to the annual maintenance contract you'll pay the vendor for the privilege of software updates and support.

Further, the costs of configuration are yours to bear, and bugs are yours to handle, just as they would be if you were to run the software on-premise.

If you do long-term cost comparisons between running perpetually licensed software on-premise, paying someone to host your perpetually licensed software for you, or just going with SaaS, you'll virtually always find that paying to host perpetually licensed software always costs far more in the long run than the other two options.

When speaking to DAM vendors that claim to offer Cloud or hosted solutions, make sure you fully understand what they mean.

DAM vendors desperate to remain relevant in the Cloud Age claim to offer Cloud versions of their on-premise software. In truth, these offerings are nothing more than Cloud-based virtual machines on which they install their same perpetually licensed software.

These options provide virtually none of the advantages of true SaaS, so make sure you don't fall for it. Ask vendors whether their Cloud offerings are true SaaS, or just a virtually hosted version of their perpetually licensed software.

If still in doubt, ask to see a cost comparison of the vendor's on-premise and Cloud software versions. If you see the same upfront license fee for both, they're not offering true SaaS.

If you're confused by Cloud vs. on-premise vs. perpetual vs. open source vs. hosted vs. SaaS, here's a breakdown to help clarify:

On-premise vs. Cloud – This discussion speaks to the deployment model of the software. Will it be run on a computer that's located at your organization, or will it be managed by someone else at a remote location. Confusing the issue is that "Cloud" is used to describe true SaaS *and* perpetually license software that's run from a Cloud-based virtual instance.

SaaS vs. perpetual license vs. open source – Here, we primarily refer to license models that affect costs. When we speak of SaaS, we also refer to those differentiating Cloud-supporting technologies previously described.

Features that Help You Avoid Problems
Most of the feature screenshots you see on DAM vendor websites and brochures are placed for their eye-candy appeal more than their value.

On the other hand, more important DAM features can be entirely ignored, just because they aren't sexy. These features can, however, help improve the quality of your DAM and the integrity of your metadata, so they're worth discussing.

When speaking to DAM vendors, specifically ask about the features listed below. You'd be surprised to learn just how many systems don't provide these important features that many would consider to be "standard equipment" on any DAM.

Spell checking – When adding metadata, you'll benefit from inline spell checking. We're just too used to having this feature in our word processors and Web browsers to do without it in our DAM systems. But more than a convenience, spell checking helps ensure metadata integrity. Misspelled words can prevent assets from being found in textual searches.

If your DAM's interface is browser based, you might be able to benefit from the spell-check feature in Web browsers.

Controlled vocabulary support – Your DAM needs to make it easy for users to take advantage of the terminology on which you standardize. Not only should data entry be controlled or at least checked against those lists, users conducting searches should have access to the same lists.

The value of a controlled vocabulary cannot be overstated. If one user tags one photo of the Hindenburg as "blimp," and another Hindenburg photo was tagged "dirigible" by another user, you have a metadata consistency problem. How many terms are searching users supposed to know?

It should also be easy for permitted users to add and edit vocabulary terms on the fly. Though you certainly want control over who can add and edit terms, you don't want those changes to require the involvement of technical staff.

Menu items and category lists offer some of the advantages of a controlled vocabulary, but they provide no control over terms entered manually by users, and they're not always ideal. Consider, for example, a single menu that contains the many thousands of subject terms provided by the US Library of Congress. It simply wouldn't be usable. Instead, those terms should be presented to users in some type-ahead function that enables users to see, as metadata is entered, which terms are permitted.

Metadata validation – Some metadata values cannot come from controlled vocabularies, because there's no way of knowing the values in advance, but you still want to make sure any values entered by users adhere to a certain format. Examples include email addresses used as contact info, and a license cost. Your DAM should offer some means of ensuring that the metadata entered or edited is appropriate for the metadata field's intended purpose.

Another use for metadata validation comes from ensuring users adhere to adopted standards at your organization for file naming or creating internal codes.

Database record locking – You would reasonably assume that when two people try to open the same database record for editing, the DAM would know how to best deal with this. But this is not always the case.

Without proper record locking, the second person to open a record will have no idea that another user is already editing that same record. The result is usually one of two equally problematic outcomes: Either the edits of one user are overwritten by the other, or the second user to open the record finds he cannot save his changes, perhaps after significant edits have been made.

When a database record is being edited by one user, no other user should be able to edit that same record. And it's up to your DAM to properly manage this.

The problem becomes even more insidious when background automation is active. Even if you're certain no other users will edit a record you're editing, a background automation task can "hijack" the record away from you, losing your edits for good.

Make sure you confirm whether record locking is supported on any DAM you consider. Also, demand to see how the system avoids or resolves "edit collisions" like those described.

Quite frankly, any DAM that cannot properly address this very basic requirement of a multi-user environment shouldn't be in a multi-user environment.

File Integrity Verification
Because of the movement of digital files across servers and networks, your DAM should be able to determine a file's integrity and later verify that integrity. Absent this protection, files that have become corrupted might go unnoticed until long after the good original copies are long gone.

Checksums offer a great way to ensure file integrity. A checksum is a number derived from "reading" through all data bits in a file. While reading the file, the checksum software keeps a running total of what it reads. Copies of that master file can then be compared against this value. If there's a match, there's a pretty good chance the file copy is okay. (It's technically possible that a corrupted file copy could share a checksum with its original, but this is unlikely.)

There are a few stages at which file integrity checking is most important.

Ingesting – When a file is first added your DAM, your DAM should be able to compare the ingested files with the original file that's outside the DAM. If this check is based on a stored checksum that can be reused, all the better.

File access – Each time a file is accessed, the DAM should offer users the option of verifying the transferred file against a known checksum. Users downloading a JPEG might not bother, but those downloading gigabyte videos might take advantage. This becomes particularly important when the downloaded files will be distributed to others.

Archiving – Perhaps most important of all, the DAM should be able to verify a file's integrity before and after the file is copied to an archive or backup.

In addition to these times, your DAM should be able to perform periodic checks just to make sure files remain intact. This is important even if the files the DAM manages haven't been moved or otherwise altered, because a failing hard drive can start causing problems long before it fails completely.

If an "invisible" failure like this starts to occur on your production system, it can be disastrous. At first, there might be no warning signs at all. The failing drive calling out for help might make some odd noises, but if that drive is in a noisy server room or in the Cloud, all those clicks and grinds will be for naught. It could be months before a failing drive's host computer starts to report errors, so you can't rely on that.

In the meantime, files silently become unusable.

Unaware of the issue, your DAM continues to diligently perform backups. Unfortunately, of course, it's now overwriting good backups with corrupted files. If your oldest "good" backup is recycled before you become aware of the corruption, you're in trouble.

Making a horrible situation worse, when that drive finally does fail completely, you're left wondering which of the potentially millions of files in your collections have been damaged. Imagine the time you'd need to manually verify each and every one of them.

I've seen an example where files were corrupted while they were ingested into a DAM that offered no support for checksums. Unfortunately for the user, by the time the corruption was recognized (when the files were later needed), all "good" copies were long gone. If that DAM supported checksum verification, the newly ingested files could have been compared to the originals before those originals were deleted. The error would have been obvious and correctable before significant time and data was lost.

Mobile Access

Gone are the days when mobile access to DAM was a luxury or even an option. Even if you won't need mobile access to your DAM, others will. Those conducting approvals, editing metadata, or downloading samples to show clients will all benefit from DAM access from their smartphones, tablets, and whatever else comes along next.

Mobile access is made possible either by a mobile-friendly Web interface or by a dedicated app that's downloaded from an online marketplace, like the Google Play Store and the Apple App Store.

There are advantages to both access types, so it's best if your DAM offers both.

Mobile-friendly Web interfaces are usually useable on all mobile devices, so you won't have to guess which mobile platform your users will favor. Web interfaces also save users from having to download apps. As easy as installing an app might be, corporate-controlled mobile devices are sometimes configured to prevent users from doing so.

Dedicated apps, on the other hand, usually offer slicker interfaces. If well designed, they can offer more advanced functionality too.

The need for advanced mobile functionality will depend on how your system will be used via mobile. If users are uploading new assets, doing bulk metadata edits, or working with advanced search features like color palette matching, a mobile app might be the ideal solution. But if your users' mobile access needs are limited to simple text searching and downloads, you might find a mobile Web interface to be enough.

Always see evidence of the mobile access options DAM vendors promise. If they tell you they have an Android app, whip out your Android phone and say, "Great! Where can I download it?" Or, iPad your way to the Apple store and ask them to find it for you.

While evaluating a vendor's (actually available) mobile DAM interface, ask yourself if what you see is truly useful. People work with mobile devices differently than they do traditional computers.

For example, when we want something on mobile, we want it *now*—not after we go through multiple login screens, database selection screens, etc. Does the vendor's mobile interface permit stored logins? If not, how many steps are required before any actual work can be done? Further, what happens if you're working on something and you need to shut off your phone? If your session times out, you lose your edits and you need to start all over again, then that vendor needs to try harder.

Further, make sure mobile Web interfaces are thoroughly mobile friendly. What initially appears to be an attractive mobile interface might later present a pop-up window or interface widget that doesn't work on your mobile device.

Here's a good mobile interface test: imagine you're in a cab on your way to the airport. The office sends a text message asking you to approve an updated file before you board your plane. A deadline is pending, so this can't wait.

Ideally, the text message would include a link to a fast-loading, clear preview of the asset. You should be able to zoom in and out exactly as you would normally zoom on your mobile device. Panning should work the same way too. From the preview window, you should also be able to communicate your approval or rejection.

Anything more complex than this is not what mobile is all about.

If you need to open one app to view the file, launch another app to annotate the file, and then switch to your email app just to send your comments, you're simply going to board your plane and later blame your mobile network for not delivering the text message in time. Darn.

But the very same thing will happen when *you* ask others to approve files or edit metadata.

Mobile access is not about shrinking the DAM's standard interface. Smart mobile design for DAM requires a complete rethinking of the ways in which users interact with digital assets and metadata. Be wary of vendors that don't understand this.

Mobile DAM is no longer an option, add-on or afterthought. Vendors that think it is are living in the past.

Multi-language Support

If you need to make your assets and metadata available in other languages, make sure this is among the first discussions you have with DAM vendors. It's easy for a DAM vendor to say they support multiple languages, but making multiple languages *useable* is what matters most.

Rule of thumb: Adding support for an additional language shouldn't take more effort than learning that language.

There are a few things to consider while determining whether a DAM really offers complete and usable multi-language support:

- User interface – Can menu items and other widgets be displayed in alternate languages?
- Metadata – Can you provide localized metadata values for *only* the metadata fields that matter to you? In other words, you probably don't need to localize the File Format metadata, because JPEG is JPEG, no matter the language. Non-localized metadata should be visible to all users, regardless of their chosen language.
- Language choice – How does the system determine who speaks French? Is this determined by the language selected in the user's Web browser, or is it a setting change users are required make after initially connecting in English? Users who don't speak the default language your DAM interface displays might find the latter option to be inconvenient at best.

- Search – What will an Italian user find when searching in his native language? If your DAM doesn't consider language when finding search matches, Flavio is going to be confused by all the walking sticks and Christmas candies he sees when searching for dog photos. (*Dog* in Italiano is *cane*.) Woof!
- Language nuance – When an American English speaker searches for *harbor*, she expects to find all harbors, if when they're *harbours* tagged by English speakers overseas. The many nuances of language should be considered by your DAM. If your DAM is smart enough to handle this automatically, that's great; if not, metadata editors should be able to easily add synonyms.

Complete language fidelity is an admirable goal, but it's not usually possible. When new assets are added to your DAM, it might take a while before the metadata in those records can be localized into every language you offer. In the meantime, however, those assets shouldn't be inaccessible.

This means Flavio should be able to be able to also search metadata in other languages, if he so chooses, without having to switch his interface language. What's more, when multiple metadata languages are shown at once, the language of each should be clear.

Supporting multiple languages shouldn't confuse users. If you need to support multiple languages, choose a DAM that provides a holistic approach to language that users will actually find useful.

Ask prospective vendors to show you how multiple languages are configured in their DAMs. If what they show seems cumbersome to you, imagine how users will perceive it.

Automation Options

It can be tough to imagine a use for DAM automation at first, but as your DAM usage becomes more sophisticated, you'll start to see where it fits.

Automation can be as complex or simple as you need. For example, your DAM might be able to do sophisticated asset routing through your production pipeline, keeping everyone informed along the way, and making sure that schedules are met. Or, you might find a more subtle application of automation to be more useful.

For example, you likely have rules at your workplace that govern how your digital assets are managed now. Your press releases might be held until an embargo date expires, and your works-in-progress might not be archived until the project manager says its time.

DAM can be the perfect ally for smaller automation jobs like these.

DAM automation tasks are typically configured as steps that human users could also do, though perhaps less expeditiously and without safe guards against errors. In other words, you shouldn't expect magic from DAM automation.

For example, if your DAM isn't capable of transcribing recorded audio at the hands of a user, automation isn't going to help. But if you have a workplace rule in place that determines which copyright notice should be used depending on the source of a file, automation is ideal.

It's helpful to think of automation as being your primary DAM user. Train human users to do only those things automation can't handle efficiently. This way, you'll be more likely to take advantage of all the power your DAM offers. Automation makes fewer mistakes than do humans, and it works 24/7, so there's no reason to put off exploring what it can do.

Use the following list of common automation tasks as a starting point for your automation discussions with DAM vendors.

Ingesting files – What options are available for automatically adding files to the DAM? Can users place files in a central location and have the DAM grab them from there, without further manual intervention? Can the DAM integrate with services like Drop Box, Google Drive, ftp sites or other locations users might put files? Can it ingest files sent as attachments to email accounts?

Adding metadata – Can the DAM add metadata that's calculated via formula, or that comes from templates? What rules are available for determining which templates or values should be used? For example, can you determine the template is used based on who indexed the file, or the file type?

Targeting records for action – What search options are available to determine which database records need metadata updates? For example, can the DAM automatically search for license expiration dates that are less than a month away and then perform some action based on the found records? Or, can it identify which files are taking up the most room, consider the last date of use of those files, and then intelligently move the larger of those files to near-line or off-line storage?

Asset processing – What asset processing options are available via automation? Can preconfigured jobs be applied based on the results of targeted record searches? Can the resulting files be stored anywhere you need? For example, once a new image has been approved, can the system automatically create a Web-friendly JPEG and then post that to Facebook? If so, what options do you have for creating the text of the post? Can that be taken from an existing metadata field?

Communication – Humans don't want to the tedious work, but they want to know when that work has been done. What options are available for notifying people about the successes and failures of automation tasks? Can the system send email or a text message? What about posting automation results to a Google+ or Facebook feed?

Integration with other systems – Can the DAM communicate with other systems and act accordingly? For example, say your organization uses Adobe's InDesign Server to automate the creation of business cards from a Web page. (This is known as "Web-to-print" functionality.) When a new employee is hired, could the DAM automatically order a set of approved business cards based on data found in the new employee's HR record? When an asset has been updated in the DAM, can the DAM automatically determine if that file has been referenced by your CMS? If so, can it send a fresh copy to your CMS?

Human follow-up – Automation can't always execute as intended. Borrowing from an example above, a Web-friendly JPEG might be successfully created, but the target Facebook account might not be accessible. Will the system just fail the job, or is it smart enough to "ask" a human for help, and then keep that job on hold until help arrives?

With just a handful of automation capabilities, you'll be able to build some pretty sophisticated jobs. As simple as your DAM needs might be at the start, don't limit your potential by going with a DAM that lacks automation capabilities. And make sure any capabilities that are available are easy to configure, monitor and update.

Also make sure the vendor clearly explains what effect the use of automation will have on costs. You might, for example, find you need to buy an additional user license just to run automated tasks.

Cost of Ownership

While considering the purchase cost of your DAM, don't forget to factor in the cost of maintaining it. DAM maintenance can much more expensive than new customers expect. In the best case, a DAM initiative owner finds herself begging Management for more money; in the worst case, the DAM software and initiative sit idle because no maintenance money can be found.

At least be prepared for the following costs:

Software cost of purchase – This is the money you must pay up front to receive your DAM software. As mentioned, this will be less for a SaaS DAM system.

Recurring fees – Most often associated with SaaS and hosted systems, recurring fees can be charged monthly, quarterly or annually, depending on your agreements with vendors. They costs cover your bandwidth, storage space, basic use fee and, perhaps, technical support.

If you don't pay these costs, you will lose access to your DAM, so make sure you *clearly understand* what you've agreed to pay. Consider not only your DAM use today, but where you expect it to be in a few years. As the popularity and size of your DAM grows, these costs can increase.

Technical support contract – Technical support might be included for a year with your initial purchase, but it's not likely to be free thereafter. (Unless it's bundled into the recurring costs of a SaaS DAM.) Find out how your vendor calculates this cost and make sure it seems fair to you.

Judge the value of the technical support you get while it's still free. You might decide your vendor isn't the best source for help, in which case you can start shopping for alternatives before your contract is up for renewal.

Software updates – Software updates are built into the costs of a SaaS system, and they're usually free for the first year of any DAM purchased on a perpetual license. What happens after this will be dependent on the vendor.

Some DAM vendors won't even issue bug-fix patches to customers who aren't on contracts, or at least willing to pay one-time fees for the fixes. I find this customer-hostile practice to be completely absurd. I see it like this: If you agree to buy 100 widgets from a vendor, and you receive a box that includes only 99 widgets, shouldn't you be compensated? After all, it's not like the money you gave the vendor has suddenly become worth only 99% of its original value.

DAM vendors need to fix their bugs and show some accountability to their customers. Sure, if a new bug is discovered in a software version that's 5 years old, perhaps the vendor can reasonably claim that the "statute of limitations" on fixing that bug has passed. But fixing bugs discovered after only 13 months shouldn't become a financial burden on customers.

If you'll be running a perpetually licensed DAM on-premise or hosted, and you *don't* plan to pay for software updates on contract, make sure you fully understand the costs of software upgrades. Some vendors charge as much as 50% of the current purchase price of the software for out-of-contract upgrades.

I suppose this might be fair if you haven't upgraded your software in 10 years, but it's otherwise nothing more than an absurd penalty to expect a former customer to pay.

Services – For some DAM installations I've seen, the final cost of the DAM software was a mere fraction of the total cost of the installation. The lion's share of the costs paid for services.

Software services are the fees you pay to those who help you determine your needs, plan your system, install and configure the software, and train you and others to use it.

Services can be money well spent, but they can also be a money pit. The problem is that while all services professionals charge about the same, some of them are far less capable than others. As mentioned, don't assume a vendor's own services department will be able to do the best work—they can often be the worst. Vendor partners are often able to do a better job because service is their focus.

Regardless of which route you take, connect with the DAM's user community and ask others for their experiences, and make sure any service professionals you hire clearly explain how they plan to help help, and what you can expect from their completed work

Software services can be extremely profitable, which is why you'll see many vendors offering them. Recall the discussion about the business model of vendors that offer open source DAM solutions.

But some vendors push services for another reason too: Their DAMs are so complicated to set up that without services, the systems are virtually unusable. To put this into better perspective, it's much easier to close a software sale if you don't scare prospects into thinking they're going to need professional help just to make it work.

So when a vendor starts pushing services right from the start, taking that very real chance that they'll scare you off, expect they have two things in mind:

- Their DAM is very complicated, poorly designed, or both.
- They're trying to increase their margins at your expense.

The fact is, not all customers should require services. And there's no reasonable excuse for a vendor to decide you need service before you've had some in-depth discussions about what you hope to do with your DAM.

Staff – As previously discussed, you might need to add some extra people to your workforce to keep your DAM in good shape. If you're unsure what these added positions will cost, you can get some ideas from a number of websites that offer salary data for your area. Google "job salaries" for some ideas.

Training and education – Regardless of whether you hire services professionals or not, someone is going to have to train or otherwise educate your users. This might be something you can handle yourself, but if not, you'll probably need to throw some money this way too.

Again, less complicated systems will require less training investment. So, while evaluating DAMs, keep in mind that a well designed DAM can actually save you money in the long run.

Hardware – If you'll working with a SaaS or hosted DAM, you can forget about hardware costs. For on-premise deployment, however, you need to think about the computer(s) on which your DAM software will run.

Depending on the scope of your system, this might have to be a pretty hefty (expensive) workhorse.

You'll also need to consider storage space and, perhaps, network bandwidth too. With all that covered, you'll need to have a plan in place for what happens if your DAM server computer goes down. Factor in the cost of a second machine too, if needed.

It's probably best to speak to your IT team and get their input and recommendations. They might even have machines you can use at no cost.

Add-ons and extra features – No DAM does everything, which is why many DAM systems can be extended through add-ons, plug-ins or other software enhancements. After reconciling your needs with the core functionality of the DAMs you consider, you should have a better idea of where you'll need to rely on extra software.

DAM add-ons can sometimes cost more than the DAM itself, so if a DAM you consider can't do something you need, and the vendor assures you they have it covered through add-ons, do some serious further investigation.

User licenses are an additional cost. All DAM systems include a base number of user licenses, but if you need more, you're going to have to pay for them.

There are two basic types of users of a DAM:

- Those who will upload new files and/or edit metadata, and
- Those who will only search for and download files.

We call the licenses required for that first group *read-write* licenses. The second group can get by on *read-only* licenses.

If possible, choose a DAM that offers unlimited read-only access. If your only extra costs here are for read-write access, you can end up save a lot of money.

If a DAM vendor requires that to specifically pay for unlimited read-only access, look elsewhere. The moment you publish your first asset on the Web via your DAM, you open your system up to a few billion read-only users.

Plan Your Escape Now

The nature of DAM is that, over time, it works itself well into all the nooks and crannies of your organization. While at first, this seems like what ROI is all about, there are a number of reasons you might one day want out. When that day comes, your fully entrenched DAM suddenly seems like the miserable, unwanted houseguest your kids and dog have grown to adore. Getting rid of it won't be easy, because others have grown to depend on it.

Here are some of the more common reasons you might one day ditch your DAM:

Software problems – Your system is plagued by bugs, or it's fallen behind the times with regard to what other DAM systems can do.

Support problems – Your vendor isn't offering the support you need.

Software sold or discontinued – Your software has been sold to another vendor and you don't have a good feeling about what comes next. Or, your vendor has stopped updating the software for whatever reason.

Vendor/hosting company failure – Your vendor or hosting company has gone out of business. This is far less a concern for organizations using on-premise software. But if you're using a SaaS system, this could is bad news. Likewise for those who have hired a hosting company to manage their perpetual license.

Budget gone – If your DAM budget runs dry, you're in trouble if your system is SaaS based. As soon as you stop paying for it, you lose access. This also applies to hosted systems, though you at least have the option to bring all those files in house.

Regardless of the reason, it's smart to have an escape plan in place. The nature of your plan, of course, will be based on the type of DAM software you're using and the reason you need to get out.

If you've outgrown your DAM, or you've had it with your DAM software or vendor, your biggest concern will be migrating your metadata from the old system to a new system.

You'll also need to consider workflow changes and retraining your users. Your new DAM system might not do things like your old system, so in a sense, you'll be starting over again.

If your perpetually-licensed software has been sold or discontinued, there's no reason for immediate panic. The software will continue to function, regardless of its current state of development.

If you're in a SaaS contract, however, you need to make some decisions, though you might have some time. Unless the vendor is in financial trouble, I would expect them to give users at least six months to clear out their DAM installations, if shutting down the system was the plan. This should give you the time you need to make local backups of all your assets and metadata.

When migrating from one DAM to another can be the best time to invest in service professionals. You should be able to find people familiar with both systems and, more importantly, you'll be hiring them to perform a specific, measurable service. Easy in, easy out.

If your DAM vendor fails entirely, again, this isn't an emergency for those who have purchased perpetual licenses. But this is a SaaS disaster. Depending on the circumstances surrounding the failure, you might have no warning whatsoever. One day you try to connect, only to find that the system isn't where you left it the day before.

Though it's always important to go with a reputable DAM vendor, it's particularly important when you'll be working with a SaaS vendor or hosting company. When more established companies fail, they tend to do so more slowly than overnight, which might give you time to react. Further, because the DAM press will likely be paying attention to those companies, you might be able to get a sense of pending disaster based on what you read. (Not always, of course.)

Another safety precaution for when your assets and metadata are Cloud-based is to maintain local backups or a backup in another Cloud service. Speak to your DAM vendor about how to make this happen, preferably without manual intervention.

If you're facing a budget shortfall, you have concerns all across the board.

For perpetual licenses, you run the risk of having to cancel your maintenance contracts. This might seem like an easy solution for the short term, but those penalties for out-of-contract upgrades might prevent you from ever being able to do so in the future.

For SaaS and hosted systems, of course, you'll lose access when you stop paying. But at least you should have time to react before the lights go out.

If you've decided that SaaS is the right fit for you, select a vendor that also offers their software via perpetual license, and who will let you switch at any time. This way, you can switch to an on-premise license and you won't have much work to do in terms of system changes.

Keep in mind, though, they won't switch you to on-premise for free. So, even if you've run out of money, you're going to need some money.

You might have guessed by now that there's a common denominator for DAM escape plans: they're going to cost you some money.

For this reason, it's a good idea to pad your DAM initiative with an emergency fund. How much you'll need is hard to say, but I would set your goal to at least 20,000 USD/EUR, or six months' SaaS payments, whichever is higher. With this money on hand, you should be able to at least partially recover from whatever issue you're facing.

Yet another "cost of ownership" consideration.

Integration and Expansion Options

The deeper into your core business processes your DAM initiative reaches, the more important it will be for the software you choose to offer options for integration and expansion.

Integration means DAM services, like metadata search and file access, become available from within other software in use at your organization.

Expansion means the core functionality of the DAM can be expanded through add-ons, plugins or other software enhancements, as previously mentioned.

At the heart of all the integration and expansion options you'll have for your DAM lies in the availability of an *application programming interface* (API), as mentioned elsewhere. Think of an API as a "back door" to the DAM through which external software (or plugins) execute commands in the DAM, and retrieve the results of those commands.

When speaking to DAM vendors, ask whether their software includes a published and documented API that you and your developers can access. If you're told yes, ask for a copy of the documentation. Even if those docs will mean nothing to you, receiving them should help you determine whether the DAM actually does have a published and documented API. Plus, it's something for you to share with your technical experts.

Integration should be possible between virtually all software systems, assuming those systems include APIs. But you might run into some trouble linking Cloud and on-premise systems if your organization's firewall blocks one or more TCP/IP ports needed for communication. This might be an easy or near impossible fix, depending on whether your IT department considered opening the required port(s) a security risk. Your IT team member should be able to help here.

On-premise/Cloud integration can be further hindered by performance issues, particularly when real-time interaction is required. For example, if a Cloud system half way around the world will be displaying thumbnails or previews that come from your on-premise DAM, users of that Cloud system might experience some performance issues.

When integrated systems are both on-premise or both in the Cloud, this is ideal. This is also where Cloud-based software can really shine.

A Cloud DAM that's got a solid API can take advantage of the scores of other Cloud-based software available. And because the Internet "pipes" between Cloud systems are rarely subject to the same slowdowns caused by bringing Internet into our organizations, greater performance can be expected.

When it comes to file storage services like Drop Box or the Amazon Cloud Drive, Google Cloud Storage or Apple iCloud, the benefits of DAM integration are really apparent. Imagine a DAM that could index files stored in those services, without having to move the files to another location. Your DAM could serve as a single portal through which users could search and find all those files, regardless of the Cloud storage system they're in.

This is the power of an API.

Some DAM vendors also offer a *software development kit* (SDK). This is a set of software tools and documentation that make it easier for developers to create plugins and integrations for the DAM through its API. An SDK is a good thing.

System expansion options, though also built via the DAMs API, are different from integrations in that they don't (necessarily) interact with any other software. They simply provide missing functionality, or improve upon existing functionality.

For example, if you don't like the standard interface your DAM offers for metadata editing, your development team might be able to build an alternative. Or, if you need advanced metadata support for a file format not natively supported by the DAM, you might be able to do something about that.

Another example is support for those valuable controlled vocabularies mentioned. If you fall in love with a given DAM, but it doesn't provide support for controlled vocabularies, you might decide this is a great first project for your Technical Developer.

For some organizations, the value of their plugins can't be overestimated. For some, in fact, the DAM wouldn't be usable without these enhancements. Likewise, some purpose-specific (vertical) DAM installations are differentiated from the standard DAM entirely by the added functionality of plugins.

APIs and SDKs are wonderful for offering the flexibility needed to make your DAM do what you need, but there are downsides to excessive modification.

First off, when it comes to providing technical support, some DAM vendors will distance themselves from systems that have been modified. So, when something goes wrong, you might not get the help you expect.

Software updates become a concern too because APIs are subject to revision by vendors. While this is always done in the name of (theoretical) improvement, it can cause problems.

For example, if you've built a plugin or integration that relies on a given API function and that function is changed or eliminated, you're going to have some downtime while you re-engineer your software.

Even worse, some API changes go undocumented because the development team changed something, but forgot to tell anyone. (Or, for some political reason, the DAM vendor elected to not tell anyone.)

If you intend to extend your DAM through its API, make sure you find out exactly what level of support you can expect from the vendor. Also make sure the vendor is willing to share with you a product roadmap that shows when API changes can be expected. Without one, you'll have no advanced notice of when things might break.

Standards Support

Support for industry standards is important because it means your DAM is more likely to properly support and work with other applications. It also means you'll have an easier time finding people who understand your DAM's underlying technologies.

In some organizations, standards support is so important that without it, a DAM system can be vetoed from consideration by IT or Management. I've seen that happen many times.

There are two classes of standards support that matter most in DAM:

- Technology
- Metadata

On the technology side, the main consideration is the database. IT departments want to make sure they'll be able to access the system's data in the event something goes wrong, or the vendor disappears. For this reason, they'll consider only those DAMs that use a database standard like Structured Query Language (SQL), which is what open source MySQL, the world's most popular database is based upon.

If a DAM's database is proprietary, there's little chance of any data recovery if the system fails. Worst case scenarios aside, though, IT pros just like to fully understand the software that's running on their systems.

A few decades ago, it made sense for a DAM vendor to develop and use its own database. At the time, MySQL wasn't as ubiquitous as it is today, and it wasn't the performer it is today.

Certain types of searches that are common for DAM applications, such as "does not contain," used to bring SQL-based databases to their knees. The proprietary DAM databases addressed this, making them ideal alternatives for DAM at the time.

Since then, however, MySQL has improved in the very capable hands of the open source community. Any DAM vendor that still uses a proprietary database today is hard pressed to identify any lingering advantages its database offers. It's much more likely that any proprietary DAM database still in use today is there for legacy reasons—the vendor simply hasn't gotten around to changing it.

Another important technological standard is digital processing. This is the part of the DAM that converts between file formats, changes color spaces, etc. Similar to the argument used for proprietary databases, it made sense for DAM vendors to build their own digital processing libraries twenty years ago. Most systems from that era still include their own digital processing modules, but I've never seen one of these that work better than today's open source libraries.

Commercial digital processing libraries are also available today. Though they can be costly, the results they offer can be gorgeous, and the functionality they offer can be nothing short of amazing. If you've seen websites where you can assemble your perfect car, including changing the color on the fly, then you've see the kinds of processing options that are possible through higher end libraries.

As the demand for increasingly advanced conversions and other processing options continues to climb, expect to see addition digital processing libraries hit the open source and commercial markets. Just make sure you choose a DAM that's capable of taking advantage of an external processing library. (There's the value of an API again.)

Metadata standards are a different type of animal. Here, we speak of a standardized way of organizing and presenting information so that everyone understands it in exactly the same way.

That already sounds confusing, so here's a way to make sense of it:

Consider the word *engineer*. Without some context of discussion, the job description of an engineer can be very different.

For example, while scanning the classifieds, you might see two job listings for *Engineer*. One hiring company is Intel and the other is Amtrak. You instantly have a better sense of each job advertised because the company association has provided semantic value.

This is what metadata standards are all about. Without them, metadata values could be ambiguous.

Granted, if you see the value "Nikon D1" in a metadata field called "Model," it would be easy for a human to assume that field was not meant for the name of the person who posed for the shot.

But what if that field is empty and it's your job to enter a value? Without the semantics provided by a standard way of identifying the field's intended purpose, you might add the name of the person in the shot into that field, having no idea you were making a mistake.

Imagine the mess you'd have if everyone at your organization started making their own determinations about each metadata field's purpose.

Now, imagine everyone in the world doing the same thing.

Eventually, you'd call a meeting during which you'd say, "We need to standardize on the meaning of these fields, because our metadata is becoming a mess!"

Fortunately for you (and the rest of us), others have already had this meeting, and scores more like it. The result is that we have metadata standards that help us keep things straight.

Each metadata standard was developed to serve a specific purpose or industry, so you might not find one that perfectly suits your needs.

You might also find you have no need to adhere to a metadata standard at all. If all your metadata is created in house, and it never has to be shared with other organizations, you might decide to create whatever metadata fields you need, forgetting all about standards. (Assuming your DAM permits you to do so.)

Standards *will* come into play, however, if you get digital assets from other sources. If those assets are packed with metadata, you're going to want to know which standard was used, so that you can make sure you understand the meaning of those values. Further, you'll want to make sure you can map those metadata values to the fields you use for similar values.

For example, say your inbound assets adhere to a metadata standard that puts the content creator's name into a metadata field called *Byline*. Your system might not even include a Byline field. But, for example, you might have an Author field that you use to track the content creator.

The goal would be to get all those Byline values into your Author field. In doing so, you're breaking adherence to the original metadata standard, but do you care? If I was in a business that didn't required the sharing of metadata with other organizations, I wouldn't care.

The trick is that your DAM must support the metadata standard used by the inbound assets. It must also permit you to remap those values.

If your workflows involve exchanging metadata with other organizations, it's probably best to adopt one of the accepted metadata standards and stick with it. As tempting as it is to create all your own unique fields, if you need to get that metadata into the hands of others, you'll have your work cut out for you. I would suggest asking others in your industry which metadata standards are most widely used.

It's also perfectly acceptable to adopt a given metadata standard for your *digital asset* metadata, then add metadata fields that you use for managing asset development inside your organization. For example, you could add metadata values for internal development notes or approvals, and just make sure that metadata is never distributed with your assets.

Among the most common metadata standards in use today are:

IPTC – The International Press Telecommunications Council's Information Interchange Model metadata standard was developed for news agencies. For this reason, it contains a number of metadata fields that make sense for news articles, such as Headline and Location. IPTC became popular for general purpose metadata use because the metadata could be embedded right inside the digital photos. (The term "IPTC Headers" refers to portion of digital files that contain the IPTC metadata.) IPTC has largely been supplanted by Adobe's XMP, which can also embedded into assets, and is far more flexible. (See below.)

Dublin Core – This standard is pretty popular among libraries and archives because of its suitability for most general digital data, as well as traditional books. It includes fields that are useful for identifying audience, usage rights and other values not necessarily reflective of the content itself.

EXIF – The Exchangeable Image File Format is the standard used by digital cameras. With each shot taken, the camera packs the stored image file with metadata that includes camera model, lens information, GPS location and more. Unlike metadata that comes from other standards, you might want to avoid editing EXIF metadata. EXIF describes circumstances at the moment a photograph was taken, so by editing these values, you destroy their integrity. This is policy decision for you to make.

XMP – Not really a *metadata standard*, XMP is a standard for embedding metadata inside digital assets. XMP can, for example, be used as a "wrapper" for your Dublin Core metadata so that that information can be stuffed inside your files. When a file format doesn't permit metadata to be written into it, XMP can create a "side car," which is a text file that sits beside the digital asset and contains its metadata.

The Wikipedia entry for metadata standards includes a list of other standards and more information.

Vendor Considerations

Part of your decision about which DAM software to choose should be based on the vendor or organization behind that software. In the 20 or so years that DAM's been around, scores of vendors have come and gone, and DAM software has changed hands many times too. Though change is ideally supposed to bring improvements, these changes have rarely been in the interest of those using the DAM software.

Choosing the right DAM vendor can make all the difference, so consider this one of the most important aspects of your initiative.

The Value of Vendor Stability

While researching DAM vendors, you'll find a handful of companies that boast they've been around for more than twenty years. This marketing verbiage is designed to impress you into thinking these companies are more experienced and, therefore, likely to be able to provide you greater benefits.

To be fair, if a company has been able to keep itself afloat for more than two decades, that says something.

It just doesn't say enough.

Digital asset management prowess is not something that improves with age alone. Without continued innovation, a vendor's age is nothing more than a marker of wasted time.

Besides, unless the same management is in place now that was in place when the company was founded, it's difficult to say who's responsible for the company's continued existence. The company's real "rock stars" might have long since left.

Also keep in mind that a software company can sustain itself for a long while on revenue it generates from ongoing software contracts, even when new sales have been in a long-term trend of decline. What appears to be a longstanding, successful company might actually be little more than a wounded beast dying a very slow death.

The age of a company also says nothing about its willingness to sell off its software properties, or make itself available to another company entirely. While writing this book, one of the DAM industry's most established companies sold itself to a competing vendor.

What the merger means for the former company's users remains to be seen. The purchasing vendor hasn't said it will kill off the purchased product, but it's not very realistic that a single DAM vendor will be able to properly nurture and support two completely different DAM products.

This purchase was likely about the acquisition of a customer list and a reduction of competition. Industry analysts call this "consolidation," and the DAM industry is no stranger to this business practice.

There's no easy way to know for sure when a DAM vendor you consider might be in distress or might soon have a new owner. But that doesn't mean you can't make some educated guesses.

Below are some signs to look for when judging the current state of a company with regard to financial health and future prospects.

Growth – How large have those older DAM vendors become in all those years? Google was founded in 1998; Facebook in 2004. These Internet "startups" are children by comparison to the DAM industry's veterans. If a DAM vendor has been in business for more than twenty years and has still not become the "Adobe" of DAM, this suggests less growth than one might expect.

Most DAM vendors are privately held, so you won't easily gain access to any true sales figures, but pay close attention to what a DAM vendor says in media releases about its earnings. Privately held companies don't usually offer specific sales figures, so there's no reason to worry when none are given. But the way in which sales and growth success stories are told can offer clues that matter.

For example, when a company claims to have recently closed its most profitable year ever, this says nothing at all about growth. Companies can increase their profits simply by closing offices, losing employees, or switching to cheaper ink in their office printers.

Likewise, when a company claims to have recently generated the highest revenue in its history, it's wise to take a closer look at that history. Was this all really revenue attributed to actual sales? If it was, chances are the company would report that as "highest sales" in its history. Revenue, on the other hand, can come from real estate deals, licenses or even the receipts of a company acquired during the year.

Read between the lines of all news you read. It would be dangerous for a company to lie in a media release, but it would also be prudent for a company to withhold some of the truth when that truth doesn't serve it.

When any company is truly growing, it's hard to not notice. Again, look at Google and Facebook.

To be fair to the Jurassic DAM vendors, it can be easier for newer companies to show growth, because they need to do so little to move the needle. When new DAM vendors come along, they often enjoy remarkable amounts of social and professional media attention simply because people in the industry like to talk about what's new.

Let's face it, this industry doesn't move too fast. So when something new comes along, people talk about it—at least for a little while.

Growth is such a meaningful indicator because companies that are growing are rarely simultaneously failing. Proof of growth shouldn't be a deal-breaker for you, by any means, but it's a wonderful indicator of who's demonstrating a healthy combination of innovation and business savvy.

Market presence – Any company can issue a media release, so don't be fooled by the sheer volume of releases a vendor distributes. But not every company can get true press coverage for their news, which is a much better indicator of market interest in a company or its products.

When you find mentions of a DAM vendor online, determine whether those mentions are merely media releases a website has posted. Media releases can be easily identified by a few telltale signs:

- The name of a wire service will be included (Business Wire, PR Newswire, PRWeb, etc.)
- The media release will have a dateline at the start.

- A media releases will not include a byline, but it might include a press contact at the end.

If the only people talking about a DAM vendor are the employees of that vendor and websites that generate traffic by placing anyone's media releases, something's wrong.

Check social media circles to see what people are saying about a vendor. Granted, DAM vendors won't have the same socially active communities that Britney, Gaga and Oprah enjoy, but you can still expect a reasonable number of followers and friends for a business—especially if it that business claims to have more than a few thousand customers.

While Googling around, also make sure you take note of the age of any press mentions you find. Are people talking about that vendor now? Or is most of what you're finding years old?

Customer opinions – Speak to as many customers as you can, particularly those who have been using the software a while. Do they see any trends that might be good or bad? Is the company losing a large number of employees? Is the user community increasing? Have recent software updates been stable, and rich with requested features? Would they recommend the company or the company's software to others?

Partner defections – Business partners can be a wonderful barometer of a vendor's health. If a DAM vendor's biggest partners are signing up to sell competing DAM software, this is a pretty good indicator of the partner's confidence in its original DAM vendor.

When a DAM vendor's partners start looking at other DAM software, you should too. (More on partners later.)

Culture of Innovation

Some DAM vendors have pushed the envelope of innovation, helping to redefine DAM and drive the industry forward; others have fallen behind the curve, selling systems today that are years behind competitors in terms of the state of the art.

It's important to align yourself with a DAM vendor that shows some propensity toward innovation. In my experience, the customers of the more progressive DAM vendors always seem to be more satisfied in the long run. Those who tie the knot with the more stagnant DAM vendors often become disgruntled as they see others enjoying fresh ideas and creative approaches to old problems.

So how does one determine who's innovative and who's stuck in the DAM Stone Age?

User communities and online discussions can be great resources for gaging public perception. One thing I find to be a great gage of innovation is to study a vendor's customer feature requests. You can often find discussions dedicated to feature requests inside user forums dedicated to that vendor.

What are a vendor's customers asking for, and what tone are users taking when asking? If you people are asking for things you'd expect to be a standard feature of DAM, that vendor might be out of touch with your expectations. Further, if frustrated customers are demanding that the vendor finally provide features they imply have been requested for years, this might be a sign that the vendor isn't listening.

You can also make some judgments on your own by determining which DAM vendors are making the most of today's popular technologies. Even if you don't need to make immediate use of all that's hip in Tech, being on top of what's new in the world speaks volumes about a vendor.

A vendor that knows how to make the most of newer technologies benefits current customers by making new features available, and by demonstrating to the DAM community that it's a true leader. The DAM community, in turn, which includes the influential DAM media, speaks more favorably about the brand. This, in turn, leads to increased sales and more interest from partners who can provide additional plugins and services to the community.

Here are some of the "buzz trends" in DAM at the time of this writing:

Video – What can the software do with video? Ingesting video for metadata management might not be enough. You might want to also be able to preview, repurpose, perform per-frame commenting and even create new videos based on frame ranges you define in other videos.

Social media – How adept is the DAM at enabling users to publish digital assets to social media? Can this be automated? Are there any other creative options available for taking advantage of the world's most explosive technological trend?

Vendors that "get" social media will have long ago introduced social features into their software.

Mobile – As mentioned, mobile should no longer be an afterthought, add-on or whatever else a vendor wants to call it. It should be provided as a standard, fully supported function of DAM access and use. And, of course, it should work the way mobile works.

Does your vendor understand the value of mobile?

Workflow management – What options are available for designing and automating workflows? This should involve user notifications, asset routing, reminders and more. And workflow management shouldn't ever get in the way of creative development.

This is another concept that's not new. If workflow tools are missing from a DAM you consider, ask the vendor what it's been waiting for.

Collaboration enablement – As "these kids today" mature into professionals that are more accustomed to make decisions based on trend, popularity and consensus, DAM systems will have to adapt to provide this new way of editing and approving files.

As mentioned, most DAM vendors aren't yet on board with this concept. But if you think collaboration is worthwhile, ask to see a product roadmap to make sure the vendor has considered it seriously.

Integration with file storage services (Drop Box, SharePoint, Google Docs, Amazon Cloud Services, etc.) – Mobile devices are making people increasingly familiar with, and appreciative of, the benefits of Cloud and remote storage of files. "Anywhere access" just isn't something users are willing to do without anymore.

As organizations standardize on one or more of these remote file storage services, DAM vendors will need to integrate them into their systems. If you love Google Docs, but have always found it cumbersome to organize your files and share them with others, you might already appreciate the idea of a professional DAM getting in there to provide a more controlled interface.

Any DAM vendor that doesn't already provide adequate support for at least some of these technologies should be considered very carefully. Lack of support might mean the company isn't paying attention to what's going on, or it might be a sign that the company is mired in other internal problems that are adversely affecting its ability to innovate.

There's also a nontechnical benefit to being a company that nurtures a culture of innovation: Industry inspiring companies attract the best employees. Though this won't present any immediate benefits to you as a new customer, it can make a huge difference in the long run. Better talent means better development, marketing and leadership.

"Culture of innovation" is for business what "survival of the fittest" is for life.

Customer Satisfaction

Case studies and customer references provide another indicator of how satisfied a vendor's customers are, or at least have been in the past.

Of the two endorsements, I find references provide the better indication of overall satisfaction. In their simplest form, references are quotes customers permit vendors to post on their websites and other marketing materials. More enthusiastic reference customers might also be willing to take calls with prospects who have questions.

Making references particularly valuable, a vendor won't list any customer who has turned hostile—doing so would be suicide. On the other hand, case studies are usually based on contracts that enable the vendor to continue to display and promote the story, even if the customer no longer uses (or even likes) the product.

Further, while case studies can offer a great way to see how a product is being used, they often fail to offer a complete assessment of the customer's experience.

I've worked on studies where the story line—chock full of success, magic and wonder—picked up after the customer had endured a year or more of misery. I think sometimes customers are just so relieved that their system is finally working that they want to tell the world about it.

Also worth considering is that case studies are sometimes agreed upon as part of another deal. A promise of free software or better service can compel an otherwise disinterested customer to participate.

References, on the other hand, are attributed to an individual, so corporate deals are rarely involved. Plus, it's highly unlikely that an annoyed user will agree to offer a reference. Thanks to sites like LinkedIn, you might be able to reach references customers directly, which can enable you to ask questions without the vendor even knowing.

Check vendor websites to see if they include a list customer references or testimonials. Find a big list, and you might be on the website of a vendor that does well by its customers. If you don't see a list, ask the vendor to supply one. If no list can be supplied, particularly for a vendor that's been around for a while, I think you can guess what that means.

You can also, of course, try to gage customer satisfaction in user forums and other community discussion sites. But to be fair to vendors, keep in mind that you won't find as many happy customers in these places as you will those who need help or have some venting to do.

Partners (Local Resources)

No vendor can be everywhere, which is why God invented partners. Partners can offer local and localized services that can benefit customers who don't speak the native language of the vendor.

For example, DAM vendors aren't plentiful in China, but the need for DAM is. Chinese businesses might benefit from being able to buy from a local company that fully understands their customs and culture, and who can serve as an intermediary with the DAM vendor, who might be half a world away.

In addition to geographic reach, partners can also provide services and enhancement products the vendor doesn't provide. In many cases, these services and products are much better than anything the vendor offers.

When deciding from whom to purchase your DAM, first try to speak to several partners of the vendors you consider. If you don't find a partner you'd like to work with, then speak to the vendor directly.

I don't mean to disparage vendors, but if you go to a car dealer that's owned by the car manufacturer, which brand do you think they'll recommend? At least with a partner that sells more than one brand of DAM software, you have a chance at getting a less biased perspective.

Partners that sell competing DAM software can also be a great for gaging the status of each DAM vendor. If things were going so well with their first vendor, why would they risk that exclusive relationship by taking up with a competing vendor? Ask them. You might back them into a corner from which they're forced to admit things you'd find interesting.

Disclosure and Honesty

If you ask some people about the benefits of social media, they'll talk about engagement, networking, knowledge share and other such things. Not me. For me, the biggest benefit of social media is that it forces companies to become more honest with their prospects and customers.

Yes, I'm in Marketing and I wrote that. Take a few minutes, if necessary, before reading on.

How do the vendors you're considering participate in social media? Do they host Facebook pages that serve only to promote their self-interests? That's not social. Do they ignore customers in LinkedIn and other professional forums? That's not social either.

Smarter DAM vendors participate in social media in meaningful ways that not only provide value to the DAM community, but enable the DAM community get to know the company.

Granted, few businesses are going to broadcast to the world the details of every bad decision they make, but when those bad decisions affect customers, those business sure had better say something.

For example, what about software bugs? A list of known bugs should be made available to you and other customers. When a vendor fails to publish such a list, that vendor is essentially saying that it's perfectly fine for you to waste your time stumbling over the bugs someone else has already reported. This practice is more than just a colossal waste of time—it shows nothing more that total disrespect for you and your fellow customers. We all expect imperfections in software, so when we find them, we don't cut and run. We just want to know two simple things:

1. When will it be fixed?
2. How can I work around it in the meantime?

An important disclosure for SaaS and hosting vendors to make is the announcement of system status messages. When their systems go down partially or entirely, they need to let you know ASAP. When system problems aren't proactively reported, you and your users will waste time trying to figure out if the trouble is on your end.

Also important are time-of-completion estimates that will give you an idea of when things will be back to normal. If you know the DAM will be dead for two hours, you can at least make some use out of that time.

Ideally, the moment a vendor verifies a problem exists, they can send you instant notifications via email, Facebook, Google+ or whatever. You should also receive messages when everything's fixed, If the fix will take more than a few hours, they should provide you with regular updates.

Is this easy for vendors to do? Probably not. But those who understand that valued customers are trying to get work done should at least make the effort.

On the corporate side of things, some DAM vendors hide behind the excuse, "we're a privately held company," when people start asking questions about revenue, number of customers, etc.

The need to keep some financial considerations under wraps is understandable for a privately held company. There are rules set forth by a company's Board of Directors, and employees must comply. On the other hand, prospects need to know certain things before they're willing to buy.

So, while a company might legitimately not be able to disclose revenue figures to you, it can certainly show you a chart that shows growth in terms of year-over-year percentages.

The value of percentages-based charts is that a privately held vendor can use them to illustrate growth and success, without breaking any rules with regard to financial confidentiality. And they give you all the information you need, too.

Ask to see a revenue and new-customers chart that dates back to the company's inception. If the vendor is doing as well as it claims, there's no reason for it not to make that success clear in any way it can. Offer to sign a nondisclosure agreement, if they resist. If that vendor is still unwilling to oblige, chances are being privately held isn't the real reason.

What you want to see on those charts is, obviously, growth. And for DAM vendors that have been around 15 or more years, that growth should be impressive. If you don't see a clearly vertical trajectory, you can assume at least one of two things:

- A large percentage of that vendor's customers stop using the software over time.
- The vendor isn't experiencing relevant new sales volume.

The math behind this is simple:

Each new customer means new money. Each new customer also means new recurring revenue from software contracts. If a vendor has had a steady stream of new customers, and those customers have continued using the software, exponential growth would be assured.

On the other hand, if customers regularly dump the software, thereby not renewing their software support contracts, that vendor would have to rely on new system sales to stay afloat. Though this would be a more linear growth curve, it should show an upward trend. Conversely, if new sales are scarce, the vendor would need to rely on recurring contract revenue just to sustain a flat line.

If customers are happy and sales are good, a year-over-year growth chart has to show impressive upward movement. If it doesn't, then the new customers aren't coming, or too many contracts are being canceled.

Either should be a giant red flag to you.

DAM Analysts and Consultants

Professional help is available to you during your DAM initiative planning. Industry analysts, companies that offer DAM consultancy services, and even independent consultants can all be found on places like LinkedIn and other social forums.

The primary purpose of DAM analysts is to take a bird's eye view of the entire industry and report their findings in a nonbiased way that, in theory, is not prejudiced for or against any particular DAM vendor. They conduct in-depth software trials, and speak directly to the customers of DAM vendors to gain that perspective too. They package all that knowledge and sell it to would-be DAM customers who are looking to cut through the marketing layer DAM vendors present. Their "products" range from reports to in-person consultation.

From my vendor-side perspective on DAM, I can say that the most intriguing thing DAM analysts bring to the table is their (presumed) familiarity with so many different DAM programs. Due to the complexity of DAM software, it's difficult to get a true sense of the strengths and weaknesses of the various programs based on brochures or trial period evaluations.

Based on your initial consultations, a good analyst can guide you directly to the systems you should be considering based on your needs. Given that a proper software evaluation can take months, this shortcut might be worth gold to you.

It's important to note, however, that not all DAM software has been evaluated by any given analyst. Each analyst has a list of products that he or she covers. Those lists will be made available to you, so you'll know who is familiar with what.

The potential downside of working with an analyst, as mentioned, is cost. When a single report costs $3,000, you can imagine how much in-person consultation will cost.

Still, if you've budgeted $150,000 for your DAM initiative, this "research and discovery" cost can be easily folded into your plan. If you're hoping to spend a fraction of that, you might be better off with finding some pre-packaged analyst reports that could provide you with some good food for thought, or you might consider a consultant.

But there's no harm in contacting an analyst to find out what's available within your price range.

Consultants are available as employees of consulting companies, and they're available freelance. One primary differentiator between these people and analysts is that consultants have rarely performed any formal research or evaluations. Instead, they usually just offer some expertise in a given software program, or DAM in general.

While you're likely to spend far less on a consultant than you are an analyst, hiring a software-specific consultant might a better idea once you have a good idea about which DAM software is best for you. If a consultant knows only two or three systems, guess which two or three systems you'll learn about?

When considering either an analyst firm or a consultant, ask for as many references as you can get. LinkedIn and other social forums can help you find these people, and they also provide discussion groups where you can ask some questions.

Purchase Process

If you align yourself with an analyst or consultant, they can take you through the DAM software purpose process. But it's still a good idea to know something about what you should be asking. If you're going it alone, pay extra careful attention to the information below.

Here are a few key rules to keep in mind when speaking to vendors, and while evaluating DAM software:

- No DAM software does everything.
- No DAM vendor will admit that.

These points in mind, it's a good idea to take charge of your vendor discussions. Be prepared and keep the vendor on the defensive. You can do this by knowing what you want to see and hear, and demanding that the vendor stick to *your* script, not to theirs. (For the record, this is exactly how analysts treat vendors during their own evaluations.)

One of the easiest ways to do this is to use your requirements document as your checklist. Based on those needs, many organizations write request-for-proposal (RFP) documents that explain to vendors exactly what they need.

But RFPs can be good and bad. They're good because the vendors who respond to an RFP should at least have some idea of what they need to show you. But the concern is that unless you've absolutely nailed your requirements, you might be asking for less than you need, or not at all what you need. For this reason, I encourage companies who do plan to draft and submit RFPs to do so under the guidance of a DAM expert.

When well written, RFPs can be a good way to initially thin the herd, so to speak. For example, say your RFP states that the DAM must enable users to assemble clips from video and post those clips on YouTube. You'll certainly hear back from the vendor's whose systems *can* do this, but you might also hear back from vendors whose systems will *probably* do this one day. In order to weed out the wishful thinkers, the requirement should include a mandate that the functionality exist now, and that it can be demonstrated. Wording like that is likely to discourage the salespeople who think that can woo you in other areas.

The Web is full of example RFP documents that can help you get started. Search for "request for proposal digital asset management" on Google and you'll likely find some actual DAM RFPs you can reference. If you're working with an analyst or consultant, they'll likely guide you through this process which, as mentioning, is a very good idea.

Once you've received some reasonable responses to your RFPs, you can set up some vendor meetings. I would recommend a verbal conversation or two before you set up your first software demo. This will enable you to personally confirm that the vendor actually does have a solution that will work for you. It also enables you to verify that the salesperson with whom you're speaking has actually read your RFP.

This is important because your demo sessions should be attended by others involved in your DAM initiative, and you don't want to waste everyone's time while a vendor stumbles through a standardized demo that tells you nothing. Some vendors reply favorably to all submitted RFPs, just to get a foot in the door. This "never say no" tactic actually does sell systems, so they use it. Don't fall for it.

When it is time for the actual demo, you shouldn't have to travel far. Most vendors will offer remote demos via screen-sharing software. These are ideal because they enable you to invite team members from all over. Better still, the sessions can be recorded for those who can't attend. (And for you to review later.)

If a vendor salesperson is local, she might "generously" offer to perform the demo onsite at your office. I would graciously decline for your first demo. There's nothing worse than having an overzealous salesperson in your face after you realize her product isn't going to work for you. If the first demo goes well, invite your rep onsite for a follow-up, if you like.

Sometimes your sales contact will not be the person who provides your demo. Find out who will be conducting the demo and ask for that person's email address. This is a good idea for two reasons:

1. It enables you to prescreen that person to ensure he knows what you expect to see in the demo.
2. In "private" conversations with your demonstrator (away from the salesperson), you might learn some things. Salespeople know what not to say; product demonstrators often do not.

Also let your demonstrator know that you'd like to make sure the demo doesn't last more than an hour. It's difficult for people to stay focused for longer than that. If your group is particularly engaged, make sure you set aside at least 20 minutes for Q&A after the demo.

On the day before your demo, send everyone a reminder; schedules change and people forget. Include the demonstrator in this email, and also include a reminder list of topics you expect to see. This is a good time to remind everyone that the demo will last only an hour, and that you'd like to hold off on questions until the end.

I think it's best when questions aren't interjected into the demo; they can really send things off track. Let your demonstrator focus on what you've already asked to see. More interactive demos can take place later, when your team has established a specific list of follow-ups.

Have your checklist ready to go when the demo starts. If things start to veer off course, remind the demonstrator that your time is limited and that you'd like to stick to the script. If your demonstrator continues to drift onto irrelevant subjects, chances are, there's a reason for that.

Very experienced salespeople sometimes conduct demos that are more conversation than demonstration. Toward the end of the allotted time, just when the audience expects to see the software, time runs out.

This is a sales tactic designed to leave prospects thinking the DAM is a possible fit, even if it is not. Once a prospect sees enough to determine that a vendor's DAM won't work, that vendor is out of the running, and vendors know it. But if the vendor can get a prospect to hold off on that final decision until a number of other equally (or even more) unsuitable systems have been demoed, their DAM might start to seem more appealing. In other words, they hope the prospect's standards will be lowered enough to keep them in the running.

When the demo is complete, summarize your notes and send them to all involved. If a follow-up demo is required, mention that in your summary. Also explain why the follow-up is required, and outline what you expect to see in that demo.

If you aren't able to record the session, ask the vendor to send you screenshots from parts of the system you found particularly interesting. For example, if you found the screen on which metadata is localized to be particularly nice (or bad), ask for a screenshot that shows that screen. Screenshots can be great memory prompts for you later on, and they will better enable you to convey thoughts and concerns to others.

If you'll be seeing demos from many vendors, you might want to create a spreadsheet or some other way of tracking the pros and cons of each system. DAM software all starts to all seem the same after a while, so whatever tricks you can use to keep is all straight will be helpful.

Once your demos are done and you've whittled down your options to a few finalists (or even just one), the next step will be to actually test the software.

Depending on the type of software (Cloud or on-premise), and the complexity of the software, this will either be a very quick set up, or a nightmare of installation and configuration pain. If the software is a true SaaS program, the vendor should be able to easily set up a test account for you. On-premise software might take a bit more effort, and it might require the assistance of your IT team.

Don't be afraid to ask the vendor for help when you need it. Some vendors like to charge for their services during evaluations, but I personally see this as a red flag. If the software is so complex that you require help just to test it, this makes me wonder about the software design itself. If the vendor then wants you to pay for this help, this makes wonder about the vendor.

If you think the software might be perfect, then you might find it worthwhile to cough up some money for trial assistance. Likewise, if you decide you want access to all the same tech support and resources that are available to paying customers, then I supposed it's fair that you pay a little. But if you're just trying to make something work that's well documented, then I think the vendor owes it to you to help for free.

If you do agree to pay for trial assistance, at least make sure the vendor is willing to credit you for some or all of those costs at the time of purchase. Get this in writing.

Once the trial software is installed, make sure people use it every day. It's easy for those involved with an evaluation to lose interest and focus on other things. But unless you hammer on that system every day, you won't get a good sense of how it works, and where it fails.

Some companies schedule regular review meetings with evaluators, which I think is great. This enables people to compare notes in a live discussion, and it also enables users to verify problems others have experienced.

At the very least, send *personal* emails to each evaluator from time to time to see how they're doing. Mass email should be avoided because responses always seem to come from the same people. You need to hear from everyone; not just those who like to type.

The information your evaluation team provides is what you'll use when following up with the vendor about what's good and bad, so make sure your team does its homework.

A money-back guarantee can't hurt either. Honestly, I can't recall ever seeing a DAM vendor offer one, but I have seen this from other enterprise-class software vendors. There's no harm in asking, because you'll be laying out a lot of money. Plus, Management might see this as a safety net, so securing funding might be easier for you.

User Psychology Management

It's bad enough that you have to play software vendor when unveiling a DAM initiative to your organization, but you also have to become a dime store psychologist too. You'll need to be able to gage your users' states of mind and, in turn, use that information to motivate them into making better use of the DAM.

In the field of Marketing, we call this *marketing*. But because people often want to see the world's marketers stranded on a desert island with no wifi (and no fence to keep out the island's lawyers, who were sent before us), feel free to think of this section as being about *user psychology management*.

Motivating Messages

Let's start with the ugly stuff you never wanted to know. Marketers (I mean, *psychologists*) are well aware that people are most effectively motived by emotions. Fear, greed and vanity can be particularly strong motivators.

What this means for you is that all attempts you make to get users to buy into your DAM initiative should support one or more of these three emotions. You can also appeal to emotions like pride, insecurity, guilt and anger, but you might find these more applicable when getting people to buy your country's own products, rinse with mouthwash, donate to those less fortunate, or protest as part of the 1%.

(At this point, even the lawyers are horrified.)

I understand this all sounds evil, but it's an evil we live with every day. Take a look at the advertising around you. No matter what the product, you're either doomed without it; it will make you rich, it will offer you a better life, or it make you more attractive.

A *really good* ad will convince you the product will greatly reduce your risks of contracting a horrible disease, while it saves you money and leaves you with that healthy glow people notice.

Your DAM initiative is *your product,* and you need to treat it as such if you want it to succeed. And that means promote it, evangelize it and sell it!

After all, you've put a lot of work into this. It's something you can be proud of, so the last thing you want is for it to fail. If all goes well, you'll be positioned for praise, a raise or even a promotion. But if the initiative fails, you'll lose your funding, credibility or worse.

Are you feeling motivated? Did you notice in that last paragraph how I appealed to your vanity, greed and fear, in that order?

You see, marketing's not so bad.

A more socially tolerable perspective in which to wrap this dreadfulness is the concept of *benefits-oriented messaging.* In other words, when explaining why a user should take advantage of the DAM, focus on what good will come to the user. Resist making simple statements of fact, or citing advantages to your organization. Make your messaging personal.

In order to do this, you first need to understand your users' pain points. Take a look at some examples:

Pain Point	Benefits Messaging
I waste too much time trying to find files because people don't store things in the right locations, or they use stupid file names that make no sense.	Spend more time being creative because the DAM will enable you to find what you need much faster, and with far less fuss.
I get so mad when I find out that an image I've put into a layout wasn't approved and I have to start all over again. How am I supposed to know what's okay to use? That's not my job.	If you can see it, you can use it! The DAM enables you to focus on design instead of rules, because you'll know that any file you find is approved for use.
It irritates me when my managers don't respond when I send something for	Mark something for review and move on with your work. Let the

review.	DAM do the nagging to ensure you get the approvals you need.
Why do people think I have time to find the files they need? When my works gets interrupted just because someone needs a copy of some photo, it ruins my creative train of thought.	The DAM enables you to work in peace, because others can self-serve the files they need.

Did you notice the "greed" appeal in each of these benefits messages? When you're speaking to a resistant audience, greed is a great motivator because it elicits less rebellion than fear, and it's more generally compelling than vanity.

For example, if one of your messages hints that users who don't readily adopt the DAM will be looked down upon by Management (fear), users might react with aggression rather than compliance: *Just let them fire me! I'll take them to court!* Vanity won't work well here either, because most users won't care about the opinions of coworkers to the point where vanity could motivate them: "Be a leader in your department and show others the future of file management!" This vanity messaging is likely to result in users thinking, *The last thing I need is more of these people looking up to me for guidance.*

If you're a parent, a teacher, or anyone else who's worked with children, you've probably already begun your career in Marketing.

For example, when you try to get a youngster to go to bed, my guess is that you don't say, "Honey, if you go to bed now, mommy and daddy will be able to enjoy some quiet time without you." My guess is that you say, "If you don't go to bed right now, I'll yank that Wii out of your bedroom, ground you for a month, and put a status update on your Facebook page that explains how you've been bad!"

Now *that's* how you appeal to a kid's sense of greed, fear and ego all at once!

Also important when sending out messages about your initiative is that you always include a call-to-action (CTA). A call-to-action is the part of an ad,

Web page or email that asks readers to do something: *Click here to read more!* or *Sign up now!*

The psychology behind a CTA is that you don't want to leave readers of your messages feeling like reading is all that's required of them; you want readers to think there's an extra step to take, and that this extra step will be the payload of value that will come to them from your message.

CTAs are somewhat magical this way. The moment you ask someone to do something, you initiate an emotional response, however mild it might be.

If you ask someone to marry you, this will elicit an emotional response far deeper than if you ask a reader to "Click here to find out more!" But even this lesser "proposal" can leave a reader feeling like his participation in the "conversation" will not be complete until he clicks the link.

As a general rule of marketing, we don't issue "nice to know" messages; we issue "do this now" messages. You want to guide your audience to do what you want it to do.

Your DAM initiative announcements should adhere to this principle. When you contact people, have something in mind that you want them to do. Otherwise, their emotional attachment to your message will be minimal, and the net effect will likely be that they've never read it at all.

I know that the topics of this section won't feel good to a number of readers. After all, we learn at an early age that it's not right to manipulate people. But in truth, whether we're parents, teachers, law enforcement or law makers, we *do* try to manipulate people.

I came to peace with this concept long ago by asking myself what I would do if I had a cure for cancer. Of course, I would do everything in my power to promote it. If people were skeptical, I would try harder, or I would try other means. My goal would be that every person on earth knew that cure was available because I wouldn't want anyone who could benefit from it to go without it.

When you have a good thing for sale, selling it becomes a good thing.

Make your DAM initiative a good thing, and then sell it.

Proactive Training and Support

Make sure the initial announcement about the launch of your initiative includes a CTA for signing up for training. It's not good enough to promise training in the future, or to say that dates will be announced. Plan your training and do what you can to put butts in seats.

Getting back to user psychology, not everyone will receive your announcement with glee. Resistance can be expected.

As a good marketer, it's your job to anticipate what that resistance will be. Because you're introducing a pretty major shift in business process to your organization, I would guess the resistance will be in the form of, *Great, now there's something else I have to learn.*

This is where your CTA comes into play. Yes, there's something new to learn, but your magic "Sign up for training now!" button should offer a gateway to reducing their somewhat negative emotional response to the announcement.

As unmotivated about the idea as a reader might be, once she signs up for training, she can let go of that stress—for now, at least. The responsibility is now with the trainer. In other words, it's not her responsibility to learn how to use this new thing; it's now the trainer's responsibility. She has done all that's been asked of her.

Without a CTA, your readers will be left to wonder what they're supposed to do about your announcement. Should they contact you? Should they start researching "digital asset management" on the Internet? Are they qualified to work this new DAM thing? Or, should they just ignore it until someone forces them to deal with it?

It's all so stressful, and no one has time for it. If you want your readers to be happy DAM users, you need to make the transition easy on them.

So what do you think happens at the end of that initial class? You guessed it: another call to action. This time, however, you'll be inviting them to your blog, where they can read tips about the DAM. Or, you'll let them know where they can go for help—users should always know where to go for help. Ideally, you'll also announce a follow-up class a month or so later, during which your DAM newbies will learn to make better use of the DAM to save them even more time. (Hello greed.)

In the first year after release, make sure you have recurring training scheduled, but don't release the entire schedule at once. If users see a list of six training sessions they're expected to take in order to use "your" new DAM, they're going to revolt. No one has time for *six* classes, but everyone can find time for the *next* class.

Another way to keep users engaged is by throwing pizza lunches during which you provide an hour's worth of DAM initiative updates.

A "metadata party" is another great idea. I learned about this from a former customer. This educational institution was staffed with many experts, none of whom had the time to deal with adding metadata to the DAM. But, turn it into a party, and people found the time.

The DAM was projected on a big screen in the party room. Assets in need of metadata would be displayed. Discussions would follow, and decisions were made.

Metadata tagging was something that few were willing to do on their own, but buy a cake and throw up some decorations, and you have a room full of metadata editors. In time, you have a DAM that's much richer for the effort.

Surveys and Follow-ups

After a few months of initial use, ask users what they think of the DAM. You can do this via online survey tools, or you can conduct your own personal interviews.

The preferred method will depend on what you intend to do with the data you collect. For example, if you're just trying to get some ideas, personal interviews are great.

On the other hand, if you need to collect data that's reportable, you'll need the rigidity of survey responses you can compare and measure. This will be necessary if Management requires you to prove adoption and use.

But survey data can also be useful to you, as the DAM initiative owner. For example, if you're measuring general satisfaction, and you see a dip over time, you can react.

No matter which option you choose, make sure to ask for *opinions* in addition to multiple choice answers. Users need to feel that someone is listening to them. By offering essay fields for opinions, you give users a chance to make feature requests, offer tips to you, and more.

Essay fields also enable you to identify your power users. You'll be able to tell based on what a user says whether that user "gets it" or not. Do everything you can to encourage and support your power users. They are the influencers at your organization, and they can help you spread the word to others.

When considering user psychology in general, remember that your users are never likely to share your enthusiasm for your organization's DAM initiative. In fact, many will be resistant to change, no matter how beneficial that change might be. Be prepared for an uphill battle that might be grueling and long fought.

But if you do things right, their resistance toward you can turn to hero worship. (That's one last stab at an ego motivator for you.)

Educational Resources

Think of your personal DAM education as following two tracks:

- How-to and best practices
- What's going on in the industry

That first channel is where you'll get all the specifics on how to do things, such as organizing files, building taxonomies, etc. The second channel is where you'll gain a pulse on the Digital Asset Management industry, so that you'll be able to better judge where the action is.

How-to and Best Practices

Though you'll likely have access to documentation provided by your DAM vendor, I wouldn't expect too much from it. The problem is not (always) that the writing is bad; the problem is mainly that there are far too many conceptual things to learn about DAM that no software manual will provide. Further, the more customized your DAM becomes, the less valuable you and your users will find the docs your vendor provides.

In fact, I recommend you never make vendor documentation available to users, unless they specifically request to see it. Instead, write your own training materials that describe your specific installation of the software.

This will save users lots of time, and it will provide you a benefit too: There's no better way to examine and evaluate a subject than to write about it. While describing your DAM system configuration to others, you'll gain a better sense of whether you've done a good job.

As a basic measure, consider the number of words you need to fully explain something. If a simple feature or process ends up taking more than a few paragraphs to explain, then perhaps you need to rethink the way that function works. (Are you listening, DAM vendors?)

Another popular DAM education resource is white papers. While some of the white papers available are nothing more than useless fluff designed to generate leads, others can provide some real value.

On the bad side of things are the papers that vendors outsource to freelance writers who really know nothing about digital asset management. You can spot these papers instantly because the "best practices" they offer are so obvious, you'll wonder why anyone bothered.

Example:

Make sure you consider your DAM system carefully. If you choose a bad system, it could cost you time and money. Choose DAM software that fits your budget, and plan a taxonomy that suits your organization.

While you're at it, don't forget to breathe. Lack of oxygen can lead to bad DAM decisions that could adversely affect your entire initiative.

I author white papers, so I'm biased; but I think the best digital asset management white papers come from people who have spent some time in the trenches of this industry. White papers should provide an interesting mix of creative ideas and technical knowhow, and I just don't see this being possible when "hired guns" write the material.

While considering DAM software, I would recommend doing some white paper shopping. Virtually every vendor offers them, and they speak volumes about that vendor's expertise and interest in education.

If you find that a particular vendor's white papers state nothing more than the obvious, tell that vendor their white papers offer no value, and tell the user community too. Marketing departments have been getting away with publishing nonsense for too long. It's time to fight mediocrity! (I'm appealing to *anger* there, in case you didn't pick up on it.)

Fortunately, most DAM white papers are available free of charge, so your email address might be your only investment.

Here's a trick I like to use when evaluating a DAM vendor's expertise and sincerity: When you download a PDF the vendor publishes, look at the file's attributes. These can be seen in the File Info window inside Adobe Reader or Acrobat. If you see no metadata, then you have to ask yourself whether that vendor really sees any value in DAM at all. If metadata is available, it might offer some hints as to who authored the document. Was it a vendor employee? Is that employee still with the vendor? (Check LinkedIn when in doubt.)

Some vendors also offer webinars that, like white papers, run the gamut between garbage and greatness. Webinars can be even worse wastes of time than white papers, though, because so few people are engaging when partnered with PowerPoint. "We…um…just…uh…released something that's…um sort of new so…uh...we wanted to…um…show it to you. We think it's…uh…really exciting and so I guess I'll…uh…show it now."

Kill me now.

I try my best to make my webinars entertaining as well as educational, but I fully understand it's difficult to *actually educate* people during a 30 minute presentation. At best, you can plant some ideas into brains and provide a call-to-action where the real learning can take place.

I don't mean to discourage you from partaking in any of these (usually free) resources, but I do think your time is valuable, and I hate to see people waste time.

I also mean no disrespect to those who give webinars; I know it's not always an easy thing to do. I just wish people would try a little harder for the benefit of their audience, rather than see webinars as a lead-generation resource that doesn't require professionalism. I think that's disrespectful to attendees.

User communities and forums can also be good sources for DAM education, but maybe not for the reasons you might think. The Q&A going on in these places can be interesting, but it's the people you meet there that provide the real value.

Personal relationships you start with the smarter users can ultimately provide you with the best DAM education you can get. I've made many friends from DAM forums that I can now trust to help me define the best ways to explain things.

For another free resource, visit the Google+ page for DAM Survival Guide. You can find the page by searching for "+DAM Survival Guide" on Google. Or, search for "#DAMTIP" which is the hashtag I put on the tips I publish via various sources. Others are starting to pick up on this tag now, so you might find even more info that just what I put out there.

Discovering What's Going On

Starting right now, keep an eye on what's going on in the DAM industry as a whole. Not only will it help you get a better sense of which vendors are the movers and shakers, it's a great way to get some ideas from experts in the industry.

Resources for determining what's going on range from websites dedicated to digital asset management news and issues, to discussion groups, and trade shows too.

DAM as an industry is pretty small, so you won't have much trouble finding what you need in just a few locations.

For DAM news, I like to visit a few sites:

Digital Asset Management News – I like this site because the senior editor is a no-nonsense kind of guy. A vendor will send him a media release that talks about some wonderful new thing, and he'll wrap that fluff story into an actual news story that puts the "magic" into better perspective for readers. http://digitalassetmanagementnews.org

CMSWire – Here's a site so bubbling with new content that you have to keep a close eye on it. Like the "DAM News" site, you won't see vendor media releases published here, at least not without some editorial manipulation. Any news that does come from vendors is suitably filtered for less fictional reading. Though there's lots of content there that's not directly related to DAM, you can find a specific "Digital Asset Management" link under the site's "Latest News" menu. http://www.cmswire.com

Google News Alerts – This is a great, free resource you can use to enter keywords and let Google do the hunting for you. Alerts can be sent as the news is found, or via daily summaries. For example, if you set up a daily alert for "digital asset management," you'll have a wealth of new items to read during morning coffee. As you get into the vendor evaluation phase of your initiative, set up alerts for the vendors with which you're speaking. It will give you a better idea what, if anything, people are saying about those companies. http://www.google.com/alerts

Not surprisingly, social media offers a great wealth of info too.

Several DAM vendors, analysts and other industry pros have started to appear on Google+. If you haven't yet given Google+ a chance, I encourage you to do so. It's really a nice "mature" version of the other social networks. You're not limited to 140 characters (of what's usually SPAM) and, so far, I find the content being shared there to be of a higher quality that's far less polluted with SPAM.

LinkedIn offers some DAM discussion groups that, like so many other LinkedIn discussion groups, are stuffed with nonsense. But join them all and see what you can learn. In time, as you tire from the self-promotional rhetoric and vendor-on-vendor debates, you can remove yourself from the groups you find most annoying.

Once you're in the Groups section of LinkedIn, search for "digital asset management" and you'll see the options available. (That link above should lead you right where you need to be, but you'll first have to login to your LinkedIn account.)

I won't ask you to do any searching on Google+, because it can be so daunting to sift through that place. Instead, if you search Google for "+DAM Survival Guide" you'll find a link to the DAM Survival Guide Google+ page. Follow me there and I'll be sure to link you to anything interesting I find. I'll also post regular DAM tips.

If you're in the mood to sit back and be "edutained" by podcasts, don't miss Another DAM Podcast. This site offers regular podcast interviews with people involved in the DAM industry. Its archive dates back years, so there's plenty to hear.

When you find other supposed educational sites for DAM, be careful to note who's in charge of the content. In some cases, DAM vendors have registered themselves some prime domains at which they profess to be doing the community an educational service. In fact, the content of these sites can be very biased.

A relative newcomer to the DAM world is the DAM Foundation, which you can find at http://damfoundation.org. This organization aims to be a neutral place for DAM education, and they seem to be off to a good start. Lots of new content emerges from this site on a regular basis, so it's definitely worth considering as a resource during your research.

DAM tradeshows and expos are covered by two companies:

- Createasphere – http://www.createasphere.com

- Henry Stewart Events – http://www.henrystewartconferences.com/dam

Neither company offers admission that's cheap, and neither is the clear winner with regard to producing the best show. They each offer events at different times of the year and in different locations. Their New York shows seem to consistently be their largest events.

Before you cough up the hundreds of dollars they're each going to demand for show admission, do the following:

1. Check the list of exhibitors and panelists scheduled for the show you're considering. These should be listed on the show page. If they are not, that means the event coordinator is having a difficult time filling the agenda. Hold off until you're sure you won't be the only person at the event.
2. If you have a relationship with one of the exhibiting vendors, even if you're still a prospect, ask your vendor if they can get you in for free or at a discount. Discount pricing is often available, and discounts can become quite dramatic as time is running out. If the event coordinator hasn't sold out the hall, they'll want to fill it will bodies nonetheless. So if an event date is approaching and you don't have a ticket, don't fret. Ask your vendor "friend" to do you this favor.

DAM Preflight Checklist

At this point, you've read an awful lot about digital asset management. And though I've done my best to remain unbiased and informative, I'm just one person. Do yourself a favor and make use of all the DAM resources available to you before you get too far in your DAM initiative planning.

And, whatever you decide, don't do anything until you're certain you've done all the research you need. DAM vendors and others in the industry will often say that no matter which DAM software you choose, you'll be better off than you'll be if you chose none at all. Trust me when I tell you this couldn't be further from the truth. You've come this far without DAM, and you can continue to be successful without it, if needed.

Do not align yourself with experts whose expertise you question, and don't allow yourself to be talked into DAM software that doesn't feel right. By the time you're ready to make a purchase, you should be a bit of a DAM expert on your own, at least with regard to your needs and what software is available.

If you're not, you're probably not ready to pull the trigger.

Use the following as your preflight for purchase:

- You've assembled *Team DAM*, and you're all on the same page with regard to how you'll plan your DAM initiative and conquer your obstacles.
- You have connected with experts you trust, and they have educated you to the point where you have no more questions that need answering.
- You've documented everything your organization needs from DAM, and if you're still not sure, you're willing to go back and figure it out before moving forward.
- You have read everything you can about the practice of digital asset management, and about (at least) a handful of DAM software solutions.

- You've established contacts in the social media space whom you can rely on as sounding boards and mentors.
- You have tried a few DAM solutions so that you know *exactly* why you prefer the software you've chosen.
- You've thoroughly planned your launch, including all the marketing, training and support you'll need to do to keep things moving forward.
- You have an escape plan, in case all your planning doesn't pan out as you expect.

Digital asset management is like a substance you're about to inject into the veins of your organization. Over time, it will become either a nourishing fuel that improves your organization's health, a saline solution that yields no effect (but still costs money), or a cancer that will be extremely difficult to cure.

I don't mean to frighten or dissuade you in any way. After all, digital asset management can become a tremendous asset to your organization. It isn't a monster!

But once you let it out of its cage, don't turn your back on it.

Sincere Thanks

Thank you for taking the time to read DAM Survival Guide. If you found the book to be of use to you, please consider leaving a review on Amazon and let others know. Reader reviews offer would-be purchasers the most trustworthy, unbiased perspectives.

The following people are among those who have been a great help to me, and/or who have made worthwhile contributions to the DAM community as a whole.

Deb Hunt and Chris Orr – Thank you for helping the DAM community see that the librarian stereotype belongs only in school books and pornography. You help people make modern sense of digital things; you are the heroes of DAM.

Andrew Mannone – More than customer of the year, you are, to me, customer of a lifetime. Your knowledge of digital asset management is outshone only by your willingness to share your expertise with others. While categorizing you in my Google+ Circles, I aimed for "Customer" but clicked on "Friend."

Henrik de Gyor – Thank you for keeping the word of DAM spread so far and wide, and for making it interesting. You help push things forward.

Naresh Sarwan – We vendors send you media releases, and you just can't leave them alone. You strip out the spin and you fill in the blanks. Thank you for keeping DAM news nonsense-free, and worth reading.

David Riecks – I imagine controlled vocabularies can sometimes be a lonely game. But it's important that you keep educating DAM newbies on the value they offer. And no one does that better than you.

Theresa Regli – You don't return my email, you never call to say hello, and you never show up to my webinars or read my white papers. But every time

I hear you speak to DAM audiences, I'm glad you say what you do. Thank you for offering such good guidance.

Hector Medina – Whether we're on the same team or competing, you've remained a friend, and you're an absolute soldier in this industry.

Laurie Cook Wagner and Will Reinhardt – We were a team, and we did the virtually impossible. I know it wasn't (ever) easy, but I always appreciated every minute spent working with you both.

Jason Bright, Jennifer Neumann, Petra Knickmeyer and Thomas Schleu – You started this industry, as far as I'm concerned. Many youngins' these days don't know that, but I do. I hope we remain friends forever.

Mom – Much of this book was written while I sat in a hospital cafeteria, two floors below the ICU where you lied unresponsive. I'm glad we decided to disconnect the tubes and silence the machines, and I'm glad we decided it was time to take you home. I was ready to say goodbye, but you apparently were not. It's nice to be able to call and hear your voice rather than have to rely on memory.

About the Author

David Diamond has worked in the field of Digital Asset Management since 1998. In that time, he has written for, spoken publically for, and directed marketing for one of the industry's oldest DAM vendors.

When that gig ended in the first part of 2012, Diamond wrote *DAM Survival Guide*—a "brain dump" of the knowledge Diamond acquired during his years on the front lines of Digital Asset Management.

Diamond has held senior management positions at Sony, Apple and University of Southern California. He is an accomplished 3D illustrator and author for Aviation audiences, and a licensed pilot. During the 1980s, Diamond co-founded, recorded and toured with the band Berlin.

He lives in the San Francisco Bay Area with his partner, Chad.

Diamond's first book, "Flight Training: Taking the Short Approach" is available in print from Amazon, Barnes & Noble, and other booksellers.

Disclaimer: Do not plan Digital Asset Management initiatives while flying aircraft. Doing so can adversely affect the outcome of both activities.

Contact David Diamond:

- LinkedIn: http://www.linkedin.com/in/airdiamond
- Blog: http://DAMSurvivalGuide.com
- Google+: http://gplus.to/DAMSurvivalGuide
- Twitter: http://twitter.com/DAMSurvival

► *After this book was authored, Diamond accepted a position directing marketing for Swiss DAM vendor, Picturepark. No content herein was added, edited or deleted as a result of this hiring.*